The Security Hippie

Security, Audit and Leadership Series

Series Editor: Dan Swanson, Dan Swanson and Associates, Ltd.,
Winnipeg, Manitoba, Canada.

The *Security, Audit and Leadership Series* publishes leading-edge books on critical subjects facing security and audit executives as well as business leaders. Key topics addressed include Leadership, Cybersecurity, Security Leadership, Privacy, Strategic Risk Management, Auditing IT, Audit Management and Leadership

For more information about this series, please visit: https://www.routledge.com/
Internal-Audit-and-IT-Audit/book-series/CRCINTAUDITA

Good storytelling is both an art and a gift. When mixed with real world experiences, they can combine to create a masterpiece. The Security Hippie masterfully uses real world experiences and compelling storytelling to paint a picture of what real life looks like in the security profession, and in doing so, becomes that masterpiece.

– Brian Ahern, CEO, Threatstack

The Security Hippie tells stories about what it takes to have a career in security with plenty of learning moments and laughs along the way. Security is a field that is all about ethics, trust, and often, finding out who you shouldn't trust. Security professionals have a moral obligation to call things out when they see them and Barak's career narrative serves as a prime example of how we should all play a role in protecting society.

– Nick Santora, CEO, Curricula

There are many lessons in the dark arts of information security management that Barak shares in The Security Hippie. They remind us that CISOs are, more importantly than IT experts, people. Drawing source material from the frontlines of the evolution of infosec, Barak shares relevant personal experiences that are by turns illuminating and thought-provoking while being funny and engaging, and always informative and well-written. Security Hippie offers a confessional-style memoir that emphasizes the human aspect of information security, providing CISOs actionable insights for unlocking next-level performance. You'll laugh, you'll cry, you'll re-examine your information security management system design and implementation.

Like other great counterculture authors before him, Barak takes his readers into new territory on a journey paved with personal experiences. Courageously displaying the good, the odd, and the downright embarrassing moments of his career, Barak spins a yarn that showcases the soft skills and strategic business mindset needed to elevate this traditionally IT-focused profession.

Today's CISO cannot thrive in an IT sandbox sealed off from the business they are charged with protecting. In conversational-but-intelligent prose, Barak explains how to think outside the CISO sandbox.

– Eliot Baker, Sr Mgr, Hoxhunt

When I first read Barak's book I thought it was about tactical examples to survive security breaches or ways you could be a better leader. I mean it is a book about all of that; you get to see his life play out through his lens, as a security special agent. Helping companies prepare for and react to security incidents. But in reality I saw it as an authentic biography about a person who deeply believes in integrity and relationships and how he's built a sustainable enterprise in the service of his customers. Finally, even his writing style speaks to his lifelong pursuit of showing other geeks like me that we can find success in our own skin. In that, I found a lot of inspiration and I am certain you will as well.

– Dilip Ramachandran, Chief Product Therapist at Nimi, Author of "Gangsta PM"

I'm at a loss for words for Barak. Literally. When I suggested that hippie wasn't a big enough word to capture his uniqueness, he suggested I come up with another. I couldn't. I don't think there's a word or a sentence or a handful of both that could accurately describe his unique quiver of skills and traits.

I met Barak nearly two decades ago. By that time I already had two decades of security experience under my own belt, and we both had lots of war stories to share. Many stories since, and I can't think of an expert whose counsel I would seek first, or trust more, than Barak's.

– Neal O'Farrell, Executive Director of the Identity Theft Council

We are all wired to soak up stories and narratives – and that is where this focused, well-organized and colorful collection of information security anecdotes really shines. An important reminder that career success in the world of information security demands not just technical aptitude, but solid communications, problem-solving and even diplomatic skills. And a little snark doesn't hurt! If you like to laugh while you learn, give this short book a read.

– Ben Smith, Field CTO at RSA Security

Sometimes a great notion starts with a simple idea. Just like in his previous book *Why CISOs Fail*, Barak Engel distills decades of experience into those "Aha!" moments that seem so obvious in hindsight and yet so elusive beforehand. One of the things that always impresses me about Mr. Engel is how he effectively cuts right to the root of things, going beyond the threats, the vulnerabilities, the technology stack, and even the business dynamics, to the people who operate across all of those layers. As he always does so well, the insights and lessons are made accessible to a broad audience with Mr. Engel's distinctive wit and unassuming style. As he says, "a good storyteller will pretty much always defeat any security system!"

– Dylan Capener, Director of Security Engineering, Box

Stories and commentary abound in "The Security Hippie". I may even recognize a number of them, with a wry smile. This isn't a technical manual, per se. It is a series of vignettes and lessons learned from being out there in the field and experiencing first-hand the world of information security (and a smattering of privacy) in companies large and small. There are strategies for how-tos, should-not-do, should-have-done, all with a dose of logic and a common sense approach to security. This is a highly recommended reading for anyone interested in some keen insights and the thought process and a rather different way of looking at relevant issues in security and privacy.

– Marc Escuro, Privacy Program Manager, Facebook

The Security Hippie

Barak Engel

CRC Press
Taylor & Francis Group
Boca Raton London New York

CRC Press is an imprint of the
Taylor & Francis Group, an **informa** business

First edition published 2022
by CRC Press
6000 Broken Sound Parkway NW, Suite 300, Boca Raton, FL 33487-2742

and by CRC Press
2 Park Square, Milton Park, Abingdon, Oxon, OX14 4RN

ISBN: 9780367679002 (hbk)
ISBN: 9780367679026 (pbk)
ISBN: 9781003133308 (ebk)

DOI: 10.1201/9781003133308

Typeset in Caslon
by Deanta Global Publishing Services, Chennai, India

To Joshua and Karma – you are my lights.

To Mia, who still believes in me for some reason.

To Andrew, who is the best coacherapist in the world.

To Mike and Steve for the Foreword and Backword, and to Brian, Nick, Eliot, Dilip, Neal, Ben, Dylan, and Marc for their endorsements printed herein.

To everyone at EAmmune, who are all such an important part of my journey.

To all my mentors past, present and future, without whom I would remain an empty vessel.

Your support means the world to me.

Contents

Foreword

I'm sure that when you saw the title of this book your mind immediately lit up from seeing the words "Security" and "Hippie" *finally*
joined together in the title of a published work. There is both a science and an art to the domain of Information Security. Barak and I
have shared many lunch and coffee conversations over the years on the
topic because the balance between the art and the science is where the
interesting work lives.

The words themselves draw up very different images of people.
Security in the context of a business conjures up images of straight-
laced, suited, earpiece-wearing enforcers whose sole existence is to
ensure that the letter of policy is followed. Hippies on the other hand
are generally much more flexible in their approach and often abstract
in their line of thinking. Combining the words would almost seem
unnatural at face value but in my experience what businesses need is
this unusual balance of seemingly opposing perspectives.

I first met Barak at a top tier startup in downtown San Francisco
headquartered near Union Square. The company was well on its way
to unicorn status. I was hired as their first Head of IT and Barak was
their virtual Chief Information Security Officer (vCISO – a concept
he pioneered). I was tasked with building IT virtually from scratch,
a mission that I saw as both incredibly challenging as well as incredibly exciting. Our first meeting was brokered by a member of Barak's

team, Elaine, and I recall her saying, "I really can't wait for you two to chat!" When I asked her why, she remained vague while flashing a suspicious smirk. I could tell by her smirk that she was sure that we would have an interesting interaction.

We met in a conference room on the main floor. The space reflected the company culture. It was a mix of industrial, scrappy, and hip. It was a red brick room with a simple round table, four chairs, a conference phone, and windows that lit the room with natural light. Our conversation began as a series of conversational volleys – akin to a verbal tennis match. Elaine may as well have enjoyed a bag of popcorn as her head darted back and forth with each passing of the conversational baton. I think we both had an agenda in mind. I was clearly trying to figure out what kind of security leader Barak was and he was clearly doing the same with regards to me in IT. We continued to volley back and forth with Elaine hanging on every moment. As an example:

Barak: "You mentioned one of your priorities was endpoint security. The endpoints all have Voldemort" – (avoiding product placement) – "antivirus on them now. That checks the box. What are you actually looking for?"

Me: "Checking the box for compliance doesn't enable good security – it doesn't really protect our user population to the extent that I want. In my experience, good security drives good compliance and not the other way around".

Barak: "Great! – we're on the same page! We can now talk about some companies in the space that are doing some exciting things".

Our conversation evolved further, and transitioned into company culture. The CEO directly talked about his concern that Security and IT are often the "Departments of No". That key facet was what Barak and I spent the rest of that meeting talking about, and this critical objective to secure the business without making security feel like an encumbrance.

As an IT leader, my goal is to leverage technology to help professionals in their respective domains do the best work of their life. How do we use technology most effectively to enable the business and everyone in it to run at the pace they need to move in order to seize the opportunity to capture their respective market? How do we reduce friction in the right places? How and where do we add technology guardrails that help the business run consistently and more effectively?

Notice that these questions are not about which technology to implement. This company, like many modern ones, ran all of its business systems on cloud solutions. The traditional boundary between the "inside" and "outside" of the company was significantly different than what had been standard in the past. Employees weren't working in a controlled environment; they were working from wherever they happened to be present. The security boundary for the business wasn't the edge between the public Internet and an internal company network. The security boundary was now the person with a great deal of work to do and with aspirations of innovating in their work.

In companies that prioritize culture people are the most valuable asset and the company openly recognizes that. People support the company culture and the community that the culture builds enables the people to do their best work. To do their best work, people must feel empowered to do that work. As I'm sure the typical reader of this book will call out, however, there is a balance. Security and IT have a job to do regardless. How do we secure the business without constraining the people?

Therein lives the art and the science of Information Security (and by association Information Technology as well). If there were a Maslow's hierarchy of needs for Security and IT, the foundation would be providing the business what it needs to thrive. The pinnacle of the hierarchy would be in building out, in technology terms, what the business needs and wants in a way that will align with the demands of the future.

And then there's the big curveball that high growth companies have – velocity. I've heard many metaphors for it. Building a race car while racing. Improving a rocket ship while flying through space. Shopping on Black Friday with clothes made from hundred dollar bills. I made that last one up but you get the idea.

Velocity is the kicker. Velocity is the chaos monkey. Velocity is the patron saint of technical debt. Do the art, do the science, but goddammit do it faster and with less money than you need. There is a point in the exponential growth phase of unicorn companies where velocity becomes the driving force of the company more than the product or the team. And the challenge for IT and security leaders is to build what the business needs at that pace. Velocity forces a constraint of not having the time to do anything twice.

Barak and I could have simply barreled along and focused only on the outcome of adding security controls to the business without regard for the culture, but we'd be missing the fun of the challenge of doing both. Secure the business while empowering the people in it. It's possible to build the ultimate checklist of requirements and then simply hold the company to that list. But what about the user experience? There's a natural tension between the buttoned-up nature of security and the free thinking of the hippie.

The science of Information Security includes common elements we would expect to see in every security program much in the same way that a wardrobe consists of the same elements: pants, socks, shirts, hats, etc. The art of the domain is in how the specific implementation is designed to work effectively for the business. What is the fabric? What do the elements of the wardrobe need to support? What should I wear today? The art is in aligning implementation of the specifics in a way that protects the business and the people in it without them feeling restricted.

The state of the art is to build a system where the natural action is the secure action. To build a system where the simple path is also the most secure one. This kind of thinking and control design naturally produces solutions that will stand up better with time even with the incredible velocity. The ideal for technology and security in any organization is to be the trusted partner – to be the "Department of How" and not the "Department of No".

Barak is the rare kind of security leader that truly gets that, the art and the science. His support made my own task easier: technology and security within the business blended into the fabric of the company. We implemented strategies that would cover critical areas of risk in ways that seemed almost invisible to most participants. Can't buy that off the rack.

The Security Hippie fondly reminds me of conversations Barak and I have had over lunch where he's shared his incredible stories. There are plenty of books on the market that cover the science of the security domain. To me, *The Security Hippie* stands out as a unique and valuable blend of the art: the truth and the lessons learned. This book is a bit like a combination of a detective novel and Aesop's Fables for InfoSec. I've had the honor of hearing many of these stories first hand and I'm excited for others to be able to hear them now. The book also gives a solid, although very incomplete, picture of what it's like to know Barak. Barak is incredibly witty, insightful, and funny, and while one might get that impression from reading this book, I can assure you that in person the picture is vastly richer. I can hear his voice in my head when I read this book and I know exactly how he would say these things in person. Barak – if you do an audiobook please promise that you will read it yourself!

Congratulations on your second book my good friend and thank you for the opportunity to contribute.

Mike Hamilton
Former CIO, MuleSoft
Chief IT Therapist and budding IT Hippie

P.S. Be sure to read the footnotes. They are like a book within a book.

Preface

Wanna hear a crazy story? Shall we go to lunch?

For me, these two questions seem to be naturally interlinked. So much so that I had struck many lasting friendships while answering them, as is (for example) evident in the foreword.

Let's face it: sharing stories over food – be it next to a campfire, standing together by a favorite hole- in-the-wall, sitting at a linen-covered table in a fancy establishment, or in any of numerous other settings – is as long of a tradition as humanity itself. Fundamentally, we are all cavemen grunting to each other while roasting whatever we just hunted over our recently discovered fire.

Humans are social animals, and this book is, first and foremost, a reflection of that basic truth.

If you're here because you read my first book, *Why CISOs Fail*, then you may have inadvertently played a part in the writing of this one. Because if there was one overwhelmingly consistent feedback I received from almost every corner, it could be summarized thusly:

"We want more stories!"

(And thank you all; this book would not exist without you.)

If you're here because the premise of this book drew you in independently, then I daresay you will be in for a treat. You see, the news media seems to have recently gotten around to the idea that security is something that is worth reporting, but with the news cycle being what it is, that reporting is, shall we say, not all that. We get the big stuff, like huge consumer privacy breaches, delivered in an all- too-familiar staccato cadence that is designed to get your attention – and keep it – without actually telling you anything.

Lots of drama, fire and brimstone, but let's face it, none of it is very relatable.

It's stuff that happens *over there*, and while it sounds scary and can definitely hurt us, we don't really understand it. So we roll our eyes at these tech people and move on. I mean, and not to put too fine a point on it, most of the journos covering these stories usually don't understand any of it either. And the people they then usually turn to for advice as they write their stories typically have an angle, often because they are associated with a vendor that wants to sell something that is somehow related to the news item.

But the truth is, so much of this field happens *here*, and happens *all the time*. We just don't see or pay attention to it, because nobody ever points it out to us.

As an aside, why *do* these "vendor people" hold so much sway? Yes, it's a rhetorical question, but it also illustrates a mindset, which is a perfect segue into the term "Hippie" in the title. I settled on it because I'd essentially spent an entire career being the bratty kid who does things his own way, unable to accept the established ways of doing ... well ... pretty much anything, let alone conform. It isn't meant to imply drum circles and flower dresses, although that latter bit brings up my absolute favorite nickname ever given to me by the people who work in my company and thus know me very well:

Pretty Lil' Princess.

One of these days, it shall appear on a business card as "PLP", but only you and I will understand the joke. Keep it between us, yeah?

Through some odd twist of fate, at some point the counterculture started becoming the mainstream. Now everyone wants a "virtual CISO" because good full-time ones are expensive, hard to find, and (here's that Hippie again) often simply unnecessary. That's the thing about highly specialized skills – when you need them, you *really* need them, but usually you don't. Still, having spent over two decades peddling this concept, which is apparently longer than anyone else has, I'd become associated with it to some degree.

And along the way, I'd spent time in a frankly unhealthy number of different places helping them with this security stuff. The end result is stories.

Lots and lots (and lots) of stories.

As you might expect, there are many that I don't share, too; I could tell you about how at one time, I utterly failed to explain a critical security concept, losing a potentially life-changing engagement, only because I suddenly had to do it in Hebrew – which is my mother tongue. Turns out my "business language" is English. Who knew? Or that one time when I lost my largest customer because I neglected to wait and ask for permission before helping them preempt a massive security exposure (talk about a lesson). I could tell you about figuring out the code to turn on some of those big machine saws in the back of many a Home Depot, once you think of the problem in human behavioral terms. In fact, there are so many stories, this book could easily be six times as big.

But ultimately I came to the same decision as I did with *Why CISOs Fail*. I want you to actually read the book. And the first step in doing that is cracking it open. I contend that a heavy tome presents its own barrier to entry, even if you had already paid for it.

That won't do.

The other thing I want is for you to have fun. Like one of my early reviewers, who also makes an appearance in the book and with whom I have spent many a lunch together, told me as he was reading the early draft PDFs I was posting to the book review board: "I was reading it in my backyard hammock with a glass of wine" – he even sent me a picture to prove it – "and it was like having a little bit of Barak with me".

So please, have a blast. Laugh with me. Laugh at me. Roll your eyes. Come back and tell me I'm clever, or maybe stupid; I'm easy enough to find. Ultimately, this is what these stories are for, and what all stories are for – to help us relate. This field desperately needs more of that.

Thank you for joining me on this little trip. I promise you won't get lost.

—**Barak Engel**

P.S. And also … if you actually read this preface, then also read the damn footnotes. They are, in themselves … quite … hippie.

Backword

Akin to a foreword, shouldn't a backword be something that one writes after having read it and is then providing a review?

The beauty of having worked with and known Barak for nearly 100 years (IT years being like dog years) is that I've had the privilege of participating in or seeing some of these stories play out. I'm a huge fan of stories. Humans are fundamentally incapable of sharing technical (or cybersecurity) information with others in technicalese – as most would fit the "eyes-glazed-over" category if they were on the receiving end. Barak and I are on the same page philosophically – when he was recently visiting me in San Diego, and I said "information of any kind is best relayed through story and song, and trust me, you don't want to hear me sing", he immediately read the relevant excerpt from the preface (so perhaps I can be the first to claim that the author read part of this book to me!).

Barak's storytelling is captivating – the stories are all relatable, and on top of that, there are implicit lessons learned that may help you better understand our crazy cybersecurity world. And even if you are one of the few who didn't learn anything from his stories, I can guarantee that you will be entertained. And true to life, the hero in these stories didn't always win – in fact, one common theme was that "business will always trump security" (or IT for that matter). Therefore, it is critically important to be able to present security, risk, IT, and so on in a way that the business understands. After all, it's about doing business in a reasonably secure manner. You will see that even though Barak has always had the client's best interest in mind, security is a difficult sell. Wisdom is often acquired at a cost (even if it means getting older), and Barak's takeaways from some of his "losing" experiences can help aspiring security practitioners to hopefully steer their company in the right direction with less pain.

While consulting is a relationship-oriented business, security consulting, including filling the virtual CISO role, is foundationally built on trust – and Barak states that integrity is essential. Trust must be earned – sometimes over years. Integrity, along with a dash or two of believing strongly in karma, is truly the cornerstone of cybersecurity – be it consulting or be it taking on a security role, from analyst to CISO. This means that it's imperative to provide pragmatic and logical guidance that is delivered in a humble or at times humorous manner. This is part of Barak's magic – and through his storytelling the reader can learn to present cybersecurity thoughts in a way that the stakeholders may best embrace the thoughts rather than repel them.

Chapter 4's theme about baking security into software (or any ecosystem for that matter) is one that we've encountered over the years more times than I can count. Sometimes disasters-that-could-have-been serve almost as effectively as ones that played out. Oftentimes the person who can best provide security oversight or feedback is not part of the design discussions so that security is relegated to an "afterthought". In modern times where businesses need to be extremely agile, and timing is everything, there's no time for engineering in security when the business is scrambling to get a product to market. While Barak's story about the company with the faulty crypto plan could be a recipe for a disaster for the company, sometimes luck prevails – though it doesn't make it right. This just helps illustrate how important it is for the security practitioner to have a seat at the table as early as possible in the process.

In Chapter 5, one of the various aspects that Barak brings to light is that security has become an increasingly specialized field which seems to become more complex with each twist and turn of the threat landscape. I often use the potato chip (or vodka) analogy – that degrees of complexity/specialization have increased roughly at the same rate as the amounts of flavors of potato chips (or vodka) that you can buy at the store. Back in the day you could purchase one or two flavors, but now – heck – you can even get cotton candy-flavored vodka. Therefore it is increasingly difficult for small- and medium-sized firms to have a full assortment of disciplines necessary to provide a multi-faceted security strategy.

One thing that my peers, partners, and clients have heard me utter on multiple occasions is that "The problem is not the silicon, it's the carbon". The most effective way to get your organization or key stake-holders to embrace security is to humanize it and to talk about it in terms that are relatable, and not in technical gobbledygook. And as Barak drives home with this book, it certainly doesn't hurt when it's in the form of a good story".

– Steve Levinson, VP Security/Privacy, OBS Global

O
FAILING TO FAIL

It is some time after the time in which the normal business day, in those long lost, almost forgotten days of pre-COVID, would otherwise end.

At least as I vaguely recall, anyway.

My hair is ... well, in truth, it is both a total and ridiculous mess, and also rather comfortable. It has been quite a while since I had curls. I didn't think I could even grow them anymore. Age brings all sorts of things, like wisdom and patience and perspective, but it sure as heck doesn't bring hair.

Now I'm sporting a Jewfro.

Earlier today I had a video call with my team, or what was left of it, at one of my company's customers. Previously a massive organization, Fortune-500 in size, it had been hit harder than most, and had lost >95% of its revenue due to the pandemic. Only months ago* I was canceling my plane tickets to the other side of the world, my first

---

* Really seems like years.

DOI: 10.1201/9781003133308-1

official business trip on their behalf, and now ... now my formerly impressive security team with ten highly qualified full-timers consists of two guys on half time, as well as me and, thankfully, my own consulting organization at EAmmune to back me up.

I am pretty sure this particular company is going to survive this, but what life will look like in two years' time is anybody's guess.

As we get on the video call to discuss our meager achievements from the previous week, I comment with a bit of envy about one of the guys' hair, which has grown dramatically and now resembles a gloriously thick black cushion.

He comes back at me for my own mess.

"I'm like a security hippie", I laugh. Then, I add, "maybe that's my next book: stories from the security hippie".

Dario (I promised I would give him the shout out if it happens) retorts with: "You should totally write that! Call it Quarantine Tales or something."

And here we are.*

A little while later I am wrapping up a long conversation with Dan, one of the incredible people I work with at EAmmune – incredible not only for their talent, dedication, and spirit, but just as much for suffering me around – and I end up sharing one of my many horror stories, an early one in my independent career. Then I mention this new book idea, and he gets extremely excited.

"You must write it!" he exclaims. "Do it now, before this crisis ends!"

I guess I am writing a new book, then. Took a lot of arm twisting, as you can plainly tell.

***

Since this is a book of stories, a personal story would be a good a place as any to start. And an excellent one to start with is the very same story I had shared with Dan.

It is the story of how I failed to fail, even though I tried really, really hard. Yeah, let me start with that one.

---

* "Quarantine Tales" was going to be the subtitle. It isn't, but aren't you so happy to know that?

Imagine this: a much younger Barak is sitting at home, laptop nestled firmly on top of lap, testing. In those bygone days, I had enough chutzpah as well as arguably sufficient technical acumen to fancy myself as capable of researching "technical things". I also had a Thinkpad x60 (I think; I have been using Thinkpads exclusively for two decades and it might have been an earlier one), which had a delightful little feature: it included a wireless hardware switch, which controlled all the radios. You could turn that switch off and then could be assured that no signal could be received by or emanate from the machine.

As a security guy, I loved that feature, just like I love the physical camera shutter on some modern laptops.

The testing in question involved a new kind of Trojan,* which I found interesting, and I wanted to check how it might interact with non-standard email software; specifically, it was a very early kind of Trojan that was able to replicate itself via one's address book, but I wanted to see if it was clever enough to work not just in Outlook.

So I set up my sandbox, and I put up my tools, set my memory monitor and my traffic sniffer, got my email client up and running, turned off the radios using the hardware switch, and … let … her … rip.

It only took five or six seconds for me to realize something was going terribly, horribly wrong. You know that sinking feeling at the pit of your stomach when you've done something monumentally stupid and embarrassing, and realize that you … are … not … alone? I mean, our current world brings a perfect example: just close your eyes and imagine yourself going to sit on the toilet while in a video conference, convinced that you had shut down your video feed.

Except maybe you haven't.

And it turns out that 11 of your (previously in-person) office mates had just had the pleasure of accompanying you to the throne. You think I am making this up? There is a woman named Jennifer who was trending on Twitter for a while in March 2020 who would be ecstatic if I were, in fact, joking.

---

* Computer virus.

I was at first excited to see that the virus managed to grab email addresses out of my address book, even though I was running Eudora* as my email client instead of Outlook. Then I noticed that my sniffer was spitting out actual network traffic.

blink
Network.
Traffic.
blink blink

How is this possible? My hand moved quickly over to the empty Ethernet† socket on my laptop, but it was indeed empty. No cable was attached. I stood up urgently, intending to run to my home office to deal with the crisis.

My laptop jerked out of my hand and almost fell to the ground, and I felt a strong pull on my shirt.

I looked down.

And there it was. The famous hardware switch, the entire reason I felt comfortable testing because no harm could be done since the virus could not actually access the network – it was solidly stuck in a sort of middle position that should not have existed, with the tip of my t-shirt clamped tightly by it, not allowing it to click properly into the closed position.

I had just tried to email maybe 400 of my closest friends, business associates, customers, partners, and many others one of the nastiest pieces of malware I had ever seen.

Now, you have to understand the broader context. I was new to this. I had a grand total of two customers by then. Many of these people were folks I was networking with, or trying to sell my services to, or were trying to help me find a gig.

As a *security consultant*. What have I done?

Panic set in.

By all rights, I should have quietly closed my laptop down, given up the dream and the path of independent business existence, and probably moved to a different state (or country). I mean, seriously,

---

* It used to be an email client. I really liked it.
† That is, computer network.

why would any of these people ever trust me again? And make no mistake: security is a trust business. Here I was, putting myself out there, hanging my shingle, and its hook turned out to be poisoned.

Come on, let's be fair: what hope did I have at all?

But I am, if anything, a determined (read: bull-headed) sort of fellow (read: em-effer*).

So within 15 minutes of the incident which, thankfully, took place on a weekend, I sent a follow-up email to every impacted person on that list. In the email, I asked everyone to delete the email with the virus, described what happened, apologized profusely, and told everyone that it would be entirely reasonable for them to never want to work with me. Then I added that I would really, really appreciate it if maybe they would be willing to give me a chance to prove myself to them anyway.

Only then did I start looking at the online job boards.

One of the truly remarkable things about what happened next is that I only received a single rebuke for my performance – and even that person did not sever ties with me, telling me instead to "just don't eff up again". Everyone else stayed in contact, and some even thanked me for letting them know.

That was, in itself, amazing.

But the single most astonishing aspect of this incident was this: by the end of the following month, I had two new customers – both of them recipients of my emailed viral affections.

I guess I was staying in California after all.

In study after study, it has been shown that most people think they are smarter than average, a rather fascinating aspect of human psychology,† that probably explains a metric buttload‡ more behaviors than are normally credited to it, which are a lot. In further proof that I am like most people – that is, I am clearly stupider than I think I am – the value of this lesson was actually lost on me for a little while.

Indeed, I simply thought I got very, very lucky.

---

* Say it out loud if it doesn't make sense.
† Also known as the Dunning-Kruger effect.
‡ Did you know that "buttload" is an actual unit of measurement? It comes in at 126 gallons of wine, which, in this new world of Coronavirus, is all kinds of awesome, because "buttload of wine" just is. And no, I have no clue if there is a metric version.

It took almost two more years before it clicked in. At the time, I was still struggling to get my consulting business off the ground. When I left my last corporate job, I was making a good mid-six-figure income; I never quite imagined how tough it can be to go out on your own. In my first year of working for myself, I earned the princely sum of $1,200 – that's not a typo. In year two, with an enviable growth rate of almost 3,000%, it was $33,000. Looking back from my lofty and comfortable perch today, where amounts like this are trivial, it is a wonder that I stuck with it. But the economy was extremely tough and I even had the honor of being rejected for a barista position at Starbucks for being overqualified.

Between us birds, I think the Starbucks people were just being kind to me.

In 2005, I helped introduce a technology vendor to my favorite client at the time, and maybe even ever. He was – is – an incredible fellow, full of kindness and empathy, with a heart made of pure 24-karat gold, and importantly, integrity beyond reproach. So much so, that it almost seems superhuman.

Mr. X, as I will call him, the Chief Information Officer (CIO) at his public company, was very savvy, and hated bullshit. He had a tremendous ability to detect it, and extremely little patience for it. As we went through the process of discussing vendors for the particular problem we were trying to solve, he ended up telling me he trusted my opinion and would go along with my decision. So I went back to the vendor I liked, and helped them sign up the company as a customer.

It was a tiny deal, about $6,000 worth for the year. A couple of days later, I got a call from the salesperson there to chat about the deal, and he was interested in what I was doing and the consulting business I was trying to create.

Then he asked me a question I did not expect, which illustrates, incidentally, just how naive I still was at the time. He wanted to know if I would be interested in helping them win more deals like this, and if so, would I be willing to sign a referral agreement? They would pay me 10% of any deal I helped them close, including the one that had just concluded.

It seemed a little odd to me, in all fairness. After all, if I am consulting with someone, how kosher is it to even think about making money off introductions that I might facilitate?

At the same time, I was struggling financially. And these guys had a good product that I was recommending to people anyway.

I didn't know what to do. So I called Mr. X.

It took me a bit of time to overcome the discomfort, but the man that he is, he patiently let me stumble through it. I told him I had no idea that this was a thing, and I wasn't sure if it would be morally acceptable to do it, and would I need to give him (or his company, rather) the money if I did do it, because technically it felt like it was their money. Obviously, as an employee there was no way this would be alright, but as an external consultant, maybe it would be alright?

Plus, I added nervously, $600 meant a lot to me. Between us, it would have meant the difference between making and missing the next monthly mortgage payment. Things were really tight.

His response was startling.

He laughed.

Then he said, "you know, Barak, I've been doing this for a long time, but this is a first for me". He proceeded to tell me that I was right in the sense that, were I an employee, this would be a major ethical violation, but then I was not an employee, instead I was representing a vendor. A consulting agency, specifically, even if it was one owned by me. And, he explained, as such, my business relationships were my own.

That was when he got down to business mentoring. "You see", he said, "no other consulting agencies I have ever used has ever bothered to ask me such a question, let alone disclose what interest they might have with third parties they were suggesting to me, except if they were officially a reseller". It was, as he put it, standard business practice. He explained that the vendors saw consulting companies (like mine) as a "channel" through which they could increase sales, and therefore they assigned a value to these introductions and support – hence the referral fee.

The fact that I even bothered to ask him about it was apparently more startling to him than his laughing response was to me. Giving me an immense compliment, Mr. X added that "this level of integrity is part of why I grew to like you when we met, nobody does things this way". And that was when everything clicked in.

When I sent that virus to my contact list early the year prior, I screwed up. When I immediately followed up to admit that I screwed up, I had won more trust than I lost by screwing up in the first place.

What a powerful lesson it had been.

Because information security – I might refer to it as Infosec or Security (capitalized) from this point onwards in the book – is, fundamentally, a trust business. It is not, as many like to think, a technology discipline, as I point out in my book *Why CISOs Fail.** This is because Infosec is largely driven by fear, a strong, base emotion with no parallel in terms of motivating human behavior. In the simplest of terms, if we didn't fear a host of bad outcomes, both real and imaginary, we would not spend a second – or a penny – thinking about Infosec.

It is really that simple.

Combine that with Infosec being a complex topic which typically requires a strong cross-disciplinary background, and it stands to reason that the people you employ to deal with it must be highly trustworthy.

Integrity is not just important in Security.

It is an essential and necessary ingredient.

It is also probably useful to note that a lot of people claim to believe in the very same idea. "It's a trust business", they say, and then proceed to sell you on something. The unspoken ending to that sentence is "… and you should trust *me*, because I'm so cool/smart/knowledgeable", or in the worst version, simply apparently "wealthy" (it is fascinating how appearances can and often do deceive). Everyone can claim to be trustworthy, but it seems to me that it takes a dedication to service and integrity, even if it is personally embarrassing, to really become trusted.

Yet in Security, I should think – especially in Security – that it is the only thing that actually matters. In the modern world, the person advising you on data security, whether they are your Chief Information Security Officer (CISO), consultant, colleague, friend, or talking head, represents the ultimate challenge: what they deal with is difficult to understand, clearly necessary, and potentially ruinous. I do not wish to fan the flames of fear, but a really bad breach can lead to

---

* … which you should totally go and buy. Like, right now. *Trust me*, you are going love it.

actual destruction of a company if it is bad enough. Ask the founders, investors, employees, customers of, and everyone else involved with, Code Spaces, as a random example.

This is why I tell security practitioners who care to ask that the number one most important thing they have to do is learn how to speak to all of their constituents, in a language that they would understand. Because Security is such an intimate discipline, dealing as it does with fear, the most primal of emotions, it is clear to me that to practice it well, one must accept that human skills far outweigh in value any technical skill. You can hire expertise for implementation of technical controls. You cannot so easily buy integrity, empathy, or, as sadly appears to regularly be the case, communication skills. So many of us in the field are so invested in the cleverness of it all that we (in very human fashion) tend to ignore the psychology behind it.

My friendship with Mr. X continued to thrive, and he became as much of a mentor as a client. He was the one who told me straight up when, as my business started growing, that I was getting ahead of myself, reminding me of how easy it is to become arrogant when success pays you a visit. Then the financial crisis happened, and even as I failed again, I experienced first hand the true value of integrity, trust, loyalty, and commitment.

It is a story, in other words, of another failure.

Building a services business, on your own dime, without external funding, and lacking any safety nets to fall back on, has really been a remarkable experience for me. As I was leaving my last full-time corporate job as head of security at WebEx back in 2002, with the devastation from the dotcom bust evident all around in Silicon Valley, never would I have imagined that, almost 20 years later, I would be running a security consulting practice that I founded out of the immediate and supposedly temporary need for food and shelter until the job market recovered. What actually ended up happening is that by the time I did start getting inquiries about joining companies full time, the offers always seemed to be two years too late; I would have taken them two years beforehand, but not by the time that they presented themselves. It became an almost perpetual joke between me and Idan Levin, the fellow who was first a friend and personal advisor and eventually joined me and became my partner at EAmmune. I would come to him telling him that I had just got an offer from somewhere and I was considering it, and he would nod and smile and ask me about it, but I could see his eyes rolling; if not physically, then metaphorically. He somehow always knew that the offers were never good enough.

In all reality, he respected me more than I ever did myself.

Still, as 2008 rolled on and the housing crash became reality, I was overexposed. EAmmune had been growing fairly rapidly by that time, and I (naively) took on personal debt in order to fuel that growth further. As a person who had few actual assets to rely on, that was a risky decision to make, and when the crisis arrived seemingly overnight, there was nowhere to run. Clients dried up, the taps were closed, and I went from earning a by then respectable $25,000–$30,000 per month to essentially zero in what felt like a fortnight. Well, almost zero.

Because I had Mr. X.

And he did something I will always remember.

His company was also going through rough times, just like everybody else. As part of the corporate approach to handling the crunch, they let go of every single contractor they had (and a fair number of full-timers as well). In fact, being apprised of this decision, I came in to Mr. X's office on what I thought was my last Friday, sat down with what I thought was my best poker face, and waited for the ax to fall.

Instead, Mr. X looked at me and asked me how I was doing.

I answered truthfully that I had no idea how my family and I would survive this. I had already reached out to a bankruptcy lawyer to start proceedings on a chapter seven filing, because there was no way for me to continue serving my personal debts. I had reached out to my creditors to try and work out a way to get through the crisis, but in all conversations I made it clear that I would need everyone to play along, otherwise I would just be robbing Peter to pay Paul. Unfortunately, my biggest creditor, a bank, simply refused to believe that I could go so quickly from the income level I had previously been earning to none at all, and just would not negotiate.

Yet even with a bankruptcy filing, some bills still had to be paid, like the mortgage, utilities, food, gas ... basic things like that. It is, perhaps, the usually unspoken part of the "American Dream".

All of my clients – I was down to just operating mostly by myself again – had either canceled contracts or put them on pause. Savings, which I was already tapping, would carry us a few months, but after that, there was nowhere to turn.

Mr. X's company was the last one that I was still able to bill. And from all I could tell, it was about to be gone as well.

He listened to me patiently, and then sat forward in his chair. His intelligent eyes reflected the kindness that is one of his defining qualities. I could barely hold his gaze, feeling the shame of what felt like the most monumental failure of a life full of them to that point.

Ah, who am I kidding? My eyes quickly found themselves glued to the floor.

Then Mr. X said "I'm not letting you go". It took a few seconds for my brain to process, and I raised my eyes back to him, the question mark clear on my face. "I need you", he continued. "We work well together, and I really trust you. So I'm not letting you go. I already made the call".

My eyes were tearing up, and as I swallowed hard trying to come up with a suitable response that would reflect just how overwhelmed I was, he got this twinkle in his eyes and I quickly (and gratefully, as my voice would have surely broken) closed my mouth.

"Not only that", he said, "I'm also doubling your contract. I can use you to fill in a bit for all the others we let go, and we'll do it this way for a few months until you get back on your feet. I know you will", he added, with a conviction I did not mirror internally.

Sure enough, he ended up being right, and that is exactly what happened.

There are no words I can possibly write, no books worthy of truly conveying the enormity of that moment, or the emotions that were coursing through my body. I don't think I ever felt as humbled in my entire life. But the reason I even share this story with you, tell it publicly for the first time ever, is because of the lesson that I learned from it. The key word in Mr. X's incredible gesture was "trust".

Trust.

And it is a lesson worth remembering.

***

A few years later, I was sitting at home, or more accurately, climbing the walls.

Due to unfortunate and sad circumstances, I was in the middle of a brutal custody fight, trying to save my kids. This was almost a year into it, and by that time I had acquired temporary sole custody, which was a relief, but I also had to adjust to a new life as primary caregiver, which naturally had a fairly negative impact on the business, because there was no way to do that and also give the business the level of attention that it deserved.

As a result, it shrunk fairly dramatically. Survival, how well I know thee.

One day, an email appears in my inbox from a colleague, Dan Swanson, whom I had not spoken with in a fair while. It was the same email he had sent me a couple of times previously, and in it he asked me if I might be interested in writing a book.

"What the heck," I thought. "Right now I have time on my hands, even if it isn't predictable in nature".

I wrote back and said yes.

He guided me through the process of writing a proposal, and I sent it back to him.* He wrote back and said it looked good, and he had submitted it to the publisher. The process from that point was that the committee in charge of deciding which books to publish meets on the last weekend of the month, and he would get back to me after that to let me know if they accepted mine.

After thanking him, in reality I expected them to decline it, but it felt good to do something creative in writing the proposal.

A little while later he got back to me and let me know that something pretty unusual happened. The publisher had read my proposal and called him ahead of the committee meeting to tell him that they intended to publish it. After voicing his surprise at this turn of events, Dan let me know that I should expect a contract to arrive in email in a few weeks.

And just like that, I was on the hook to deliver a manuscript, right in the middle of the most challenging personal crisis I had ever dealt with, and while struggling to survive.

Did I mention that I had given myself four months to complete it?† Talk about setting myself up for a fall.

Initially, it sure seemed destined to fail. It took me almost two months to get anything sensible written at all, and even that felt unnatural and, worse, read that way. The four people I trusted to read

---

* As you may have guessed already, this was the genesis of *Why CISOs Fail*.

† Incidentally, I made a similar mistake with this book. Apparently, I can't learn this particular lesson.

through it and give me feedback all came back in the space of 72 hours to let me know in no uncertain terms that it wasn't any good. The common theme? "You're not an academic, so stop pretending to be one. Just start over and write like you speak, that's what everybody loves".

Awash in the warm embrace of another failure, I started over, and wrote the way I speak. And boy, did it flow.

By that time, the court has arranged it so the kids would go on supervised visits twice a week, for three hours at a time. I would take them there, and then I would sit in the Starbucks nearby to wait out the appointment. What ended up happening is that I took those precious hours and called them "book time", and basically wrote the entire thing that way: in three-hour increments, in the same seat, by the same window, at the same Starbucks location.

When I delivered the final manuscript, it was only a month late. It took the publisher longer to actually get the book into print than it took me to write it.

I still have a nagging feeling that the odds were stacked fairly heavily against such an outcome ever coming to fruition.

***

Indeed, this is a book of stories. Because of the somewhat unusual path I have followed in my career in the field of information security to this point, I have encountered a surprisingly large variety of anecdotes, situations, and tales in the field. It comes with the territory of carving out a niche for serving as the Head of Security or CISO for multiple companies at once, and doing it for a fair bit of time. What I will also do, as I have attempted above, is share with you the lessons I personally took from each of these stories. You may well disagree with my conclusions, and draw your own, but at the very least, I hope to hit my primary goal, which is to entertain you along the way.

Each of the following chapters and stories therein will roughly revolve around a particular aspect of the discipline. This can help provide some structure, so that in the future if you run across a situation that reminds you of one of these stories, it might perhaps make it easier to find it.* Since it is my firm belief that Security is a standalone business discipline, with its core being about people and their

---

* Look at me being all pretentious and expecting that you would continue to refer to this book in the future.

behaviors, the experiences I will be sharing with you will reflect that belief, and rather strongly at that.

It is perhaps useful to note that the stories I opted to include in this text are, by and large, not earth-shattering – they primarily constitute, instead, of "inside baseball" in the associated organizations. It is my contention that there are always books (and other reporting) that cover the sensational stuff, but you rarely (if ever) find ones that cover the "daily crazy" that happens all over the place, and all too often, all at once. Some of these may have hit the news, but if they did, it would have been in a minor way and you are most likely never going to remember them.

But they do share a trait, which is this: all of them represent situations that are far more common than we like to think. It is my hope that, as you read this book, you will come across one or more that will sound oddly familiar to you, and as a consequence, we can have a virtual laugh together while I share my perspective with you; and if I'm really lucky, that perspective will help illuminate things for you in a new and interesting way.

These stories are, in other words, relatable.

Every single one of the stories is real. It actually happened, I was there. As you might expect, I will not be naming names (unless otherwise allowed to by the relevant parties, at which point I will state so), and I will be changing the details to a degree in order to support plausible deniability. For the most part, any names of the people involved that I do use in this book will be made up. The industry to which the companies may belong may also be changed, as will some of the details. In other words, my goal is to dissuade you from trying to guess who might have really been involved.

I still work in this field, and have no desire to embarrass anyone – that is, except myself, which, to be fair, happens quite naturally.

What better way to begin, then, than to transition right into the stuff of nightmares? When the bad guys come, surviving the experience is only half of the story. It takes its toll long after the originating event has concluded. Actually learning from it can be stressful, and present an emotional and mental challenge.

So let's start right there.

Because if there is one thing a "multiple offender" many times over in the role of CISO* can tell you, the idea that events like this don't come with a heavy emotional price is ridiculous. The idea that you can always fend them off successfully is even more so.

---

* Me. So are the men in white coming to pick me up soon?

1

THEY BE COMIN' AFTER YA

In recent years, there has been more and more of a public discussion about the need to learn how to embrace failure. Silicon Valley has even coined a neat terminology around it, and the notion of "failing fast" has found its way into many a technology company's vision statement. As long as you learn from it, then, the thinking goes, it does not really count as failure.

Which is all well and fine in technology development, but if said failure results in, oh, the loss of the entire business, then one might reasonably argue that doing it quickly would perhaps be a tad less valuable, rather than more.

In other words, the notion is limited to certain aspects of the business. Typically it reflects the idea that when trying new things, it is better to try a lot of them and rapidly discard the ones that do not work as one would have hoped. Like throwing spaghetti at the wall, "failing fast" in such environments can dramatically increase innovation (or, if managed poorly, chaos, which in itself is an interesting failure mode worthy of an entire book – one probably written by somebody else). This sort of continued iteration can help uncover good ideas that could have significant market value and, just as importantly, avoid large investments in blind alleys that end up leading nowhere.

One big underlying assumption here is, of course, that this sort of thing is usually very much confined to a lab setting. The exposure to this "engineered failure" process is pretty much limited to research and development budgets, which allows it to be fairly contained, and those costs are quickly repaid once something sticks (to that proverbial wall).

It's smart business, really.

But what if we try to take this idea and apply it to the realm of technology operations?

DOI: 10.1201/9781003133308-2

It is not as crazy as it sounds, actually. One of the best emerging concepts in Security is that of "cyber resilience", a term used to describe an environment built to withstand and contain as many failure modes as possible and in such a fashion that it can be brought back up quickly. In their book *The Fifth Domain*, Richard Clarke and Robert Knake discuss this idea at length, doing so in very grand terms that, in addition to applying to large enterprises, also pertain to the largest scale of operations we humans have ever created – national governments.

The idea itself is simple enough. One of the truisms of security is that you simply cannot build a system that will successfully prevent all attacks. It is not actually possible, and anyone who claims otherwise is trying to sell you something (I'm looking at you, security product and services vendors). There are many reasons for why this is true, but let me state the most obvious, the one about asymmetric warfare: in the world of security, the defender has to be right every time, whereas the attacker only has to be right once. And when the battle itself takes place over copper and fiber wiring, with no actual troops to deploy or supply lines to maintain,* and at little to no cost to the attacking army, time itself dictates that a determined enough party will ultimately succeed.

So instead of only trying to prevent bad things from happening, the thinking behind cyber resilience is that we do what we reasonably can to stop malicious parties, to delay the impact of their actions, to alert us as quickly as possible that damage is accruing, and to have mechanisms in place to recover quickly and minimize the overall disruption. This is effective due to many reasons, but let me again state the obvious one: the cost of recovery in a well-prepared organization is dramatically reduced for the defender, and the equation actually flips around if properly executed. This is true because of the value of time; rapid recovery resets the clock for the attacker, who now has to again spend all the time and effort to find a new way through, if they are so inclined, while the defender is back to normal operations and has already plugged the holes that allowed the initial attempt to succeed. If the environment is resilient enough, then this delay and repeat sequence can fairly reliably be estimated in weeks or months.

---

* Caffeine and candy notwithstanding.

The attacker, unless particularly determined (and it is then a completely different matter than what one usually encounters in the private sector), will hopefully end up frustrated and choose to go after an easier target.

Alright, this was already a longer intro to this chapter than I planned for.

Story time.

***

Back in the Oughts, I knew someone who was a very strong technical security person. He lived in a different country, one that once was but is no longer part of the EU,* and he got a job offer from a large financial institution, the details of which I have never seen before, nor since.

The role itself was director of IT security (the title "Chief Information Security Officer (CISO)" had not become popular yet, and the field was still overwhelmingly viewed as a technology one focused around network and system administration). The job paid well enough, at the equivalent of about $200,000 per year, but that was not what made it interesting.

What did was the fascinating "success or failure clause" baked into it. It was really simple, and worked like this: over each period of 12 calendar months during his employment, there was one single measurement of success – or failure. If a certain set of systems were not breached, fully or partially (including even minor sensitive data leaks), during that time period, then he would receive a bonus. If they were, then he would not get the bonus (and, let's be fair, he would also most likely lose his job).

The bonus itself was what made it remarkable, in that it amounted to about $1,000,000.

I have lost touch with the fellow since then, unfortunately, but I do know that he did not sleep much in the first year of this contract.

Amazing stuff, really, and other than the shock value (for me, anyway), utterly meaningless from a security perspective. Because while it seems like an excellent way to motivate someone to do the best they

---

* How's that for hiding incriminating detail? I mean, there is *no way* you would *ever* be able to guess to which country I am referring. I am so smart!

can (and potentially give them the biggest ulcers ever recorded), it ignores the fact that breaches are often a matter of luck rather than effort, and the reality is captured by the well-known adage about *if someone wants to get you badly enough, they will*. More importantly, the question remains: say the worst did happen. Other than saving themselves the cost of the bonus for that year, how would this change the final outcome for the financial institution, beyond having someone to readily fire?*

In this vein, there is another story that I would like to share with respect to one of my own customers. We shall call him Dudley.†

It was a Thursday evening, one week before Thanksgiving, and I was in Dallas attending my favorite conference, as I do every year.‡ A new event was about to start when my phone lit up with an incoming call from Dudley, and because he was an important client, I stepped aside to a relatively quiet corner and picked it up.

"Barak, listen. I would never bother you like this except I really need you to help me figure something out". He knew this was my "break time" and how essential it was to my mental stability, and so I knew this had to be important.

"I got this weird incoming message on LinkedIn from some company in Europe I never heard of, who said they may have seen chatter about our company being targeted by hackers, and I don't know what to make of it".

"Is it from someone you know or a complete stranger?" I asked.

"Stranger. But they said they knew our CEO".

"Did they give you any information at all beyond that intro?"

"No. They said I should reach out to them if I wanted to get it".

---

* Let's be honest; they would fire the security leader anyway. It is one of the unspoken and sad truths about being a CISO in an organization that views it as a "defensive role" – if the walls crumble, it is their head that rolls. For one thing, it allows everyone else to save face.

† Of course the name is made up. I told you I was going to do that. Plus I like Dudley. It is such a cool name. Dudley. Dudley. Woot!

‡ See if you can guess which conference it is by doing some Internet sleuthing. I will give you a hint: it has nothing at all to do with security, and everything to do with my favorite hobby. If you figure it out, and are so inclined, write to me on LinkedIn and tell me what my "handle" is for this conference, which matches the one I use on the sponsoring organization's website.

"Sounds like some elaborate social engineering deal to me", I mused. But it sounded like nothing I had ever heard before. We agreed that he would ask them for more information, and also verify with the CEO their claim of knowing him, and we can talk about it again. We hung up and I went back to the event.

You will note that my own response was mostly suspicious, rather than alarmed. I am not patting myself on the back here, because it turns out that the reach out was indeed legitimate, came from a player in the extremely new (back then) commercial threat intelligence field, and was completely honest in that the only reason they did it and offered Dudley this valuable insight for free was because their CEO knew the CEO of Dudley's company personally.

In other words, I initially read this all wrong. To be even more candid, being where I was, my desire to get back to my fun activities was also extremely strong, probably further reinforcing my tendency to initially view this message as suspect. I really, really *didn't want it to be real*, and I therefore quickly determined that it likely wasn't real, thereby mirroring the decision making process made by many before me (and many more since and forever more) when a crisis was unfolding in front of their very eyes. My highly developed "gut sense" failed me, and as a result, I almost failed Dudley.

Well, the conference pretty much ended for me that night.

By the next day and throughout the weekend I was on conference calls with the team back in San Francisco figuring out actions to take against the developing attack.

But here is why I love sharing this story.

Ready?

We had, at his company, implemented a fairly robust system of operational controls that would both alert us to unusual events in a timely manner, but also make it a bit harder for anyone to do real damage without hitting a lot of obstacles. And more importantly, to recover fairly quickly in the event something bad happened.

Cyber resilience.

This next point is worth stressing: for the following week, *Dudley's team was fighting a group of for-profit professional hackers in real time over control of their systems.* Red team vs. blue team, unfolding in real life, just like in the movies. Putting everything else aside, this in itself is the sort of mad scenario one rarely if ever gets an opportunity to experience, when there is something tangible on the line. Anyhow, the team lost some battles, won others, and crucially, managed to keep the critical bits going even as they were being targeted to be stolen or taken down (as the hackers clearly became angry, they just started shutting stuff off, seemingly out of spite).

Personally, I felt both helpless and humbled. When this happens to you, the last thing you are thinking about is "look at us still going because we had a great plan for dealing with this kind of event". It is easy to fall into despair, but I had to continue to provide advice and guidance to the organization. And I could see the future: the company would end up in the news, and I would lose even the little credibility I may have gained in the industry as a result.

Hey, I'm nothing if not easy on myself.

The following Friday, two US Secret Service (USSS) agents showed up at the office where we all were, asking to talk to whomever was in charge. Dudley ultimately asked me to chat with them so as not to distract his team, who were by then hunting down any remnants of the attack that might still be in the environment. The end result was remarkable; when they left, the lead agent handed me his card and asked that when it was all over, maybe we could reach out to them and give them the rundown of what had happened, because, as he put it to me, "we never had a case where the company dealt with this in real time. It is pretty much always months after the fact. We want to learn from what you did".

Let me repeat that.

"We want to learn from what you did".

And with that simple statement, my spirits were lifted.

I spent quite a bit of time with Dudley figuring out the media angle to this, and the company did end up in the news, but because the damage was ultimately extremely small due to the way they were prepared and responded, it did not cause the kind of waves that some of the larger, far more well-known breaches did.

All in all, it was a beautiful failure.

Another fascinating aspect of this story comes from a phone conference I was a silent party to about nine months later. Because Dudley's company had payment card industry (PCI) responsibilities, VISA had assigned an external PCI auditor, one of the largest in the country, to go and inspect the systems post-breach to find out what went wrong in terms of PCI compliance.

Because we all know that being compliant means being secure.*

Much to their surprise (and, frankly, mine), they could not find anything. The company was indeed compliant at the time of the breach, and was taken by a group of professional hackers deploying zero-day[†] techniques that were targeting them explicitly. In other words, it was living proof of the very same principle we discussed earlier: that you can't completely prevent a determined enough attacker from getting in.

The bad guys really wanted in, and so they got in.

I was a recipient of all the reports, and the first one basically stated just that – there was nothing wrong, no control failure that led to this, just plain bad luck.

The problem was that this auditing company and VISA were just about to release a huge report with a very specific message: that no company ever known to be breached was ever actually compliant with PCI at the time that it happened, regardless of their formal compliance status. I can't actually fault their intent; this was still during PCI's relatively early days, and VISA was trying to get people to do more, do better, and do it more quickly. This report would be a nudge in the right direction.

Except that here was living proof that it was not entirely true.

This led to some fascinating emails back and forth that I was also privy to as the company's "security person", and ultimately to that conference call, and to a moment that I will never forget.

The national lead auditor for the auditing firm stated again that they could not find anything materially wrong with the company's PCI compliance posture, whereas the person on the call representing VISA almost barked back: "well, find something! We can't let this happen!"

I was, and still am to this day, extremely glad I had myself on mute.

Following the call, the final breach report showed two elements in one of the sections where the lead auditor changed the answer from

---

* I know you know I am being sarcastic … right?

† This is a term in the field indicating a type of technical vulnerability that is not yet publicly known – the most valuable kind from an attacker's perspective, because no defenses have been designed to mitigate it yet.

"no evidence found" (of a failed control) to "inconclusive", with the note being that it was not completely clear if everything had worked properly, that is, that they could not prove conclusively that those controls had not failed.*

The bigger marketing report, about how no company was ever found in compliance with PCI at the time of the breach, could be and was issued on schedule, and as far as I can tell, had the positive impact everyone was aiming for, in that retailers started taking PCI compliance a wee bit more seriously.

Perhaps amusingly, in tacit acknowledgment of the truth of the matter, Dudley's company continued to run its own PCI audits in subsequent years. They were spared the burden of having an auditor assigned by VISA for a certain number of years, as is normally the case in these breach situations. They also got a minuscule slap on the wrist kind of fine,† but that was the extent of the enforcement actions.

As a side note, I want to make sure this does not sound like a criticism of VISA; their efforts (and do not let anyone tell you otherwise, VISA is and has been the primary driver behind retail merchant security and PCI, and the other associations have essentially been tagging along) have resulted in increased security for everyone, companies and consumers alike. It is just that this event came at an unfortunate point in time, as they so often do. Personally, and the amusement value notwithstanding, I think it was handled quite well, at least from my (thankfully muted) fly on the wall position.

Other companies, as we well know from the news, do not usually fare quite so well.

***

I am reminded of another situation in which I got to encounter the folks from the USSS San Francisco office. Acting in the role of CISO for one of our customers, I was informed that they had reached out to us asking to come and visit, because it looked to them like the company was somehow involved in a huge retail breach – it was the largest known such successful attack in history at that time.

---

* We have a phrase in Hebrew to describe this sort of twisted logic, which translates loosely to "go prove you don't have a sister". I will let you play around with this in your mind. Enjoy.
† $5,000, IIRC.

And yes, you did hear about it, guaranteed.

I was, of course, curious. There was no obvious connection between our organization and the one that was breached (let us call them "Victim Company"), and no indication anywhere in our own logs and audit trails that we were ever somehow a part of it. Yet the secret service guys insisted. They came and told us that the logs from the breached systems clearly showed that the leaked files were placed on a file storage system within our Internet address (IP) space, and they wanted access to that file store and its associated logs.

They gave us a hard drive onto which they wanted us to download everything, which is pretty normal and how you start creating a proper chain of evidence.

We were happy to oblige.

Except that there was a problem.

Such a system never existed in our environment.*

It was quite mysterious; on one hand, these guys told us that back in headquarters, their analysis was 100% accurate, and the IP definitely belonged to us. At the same time, the system they claimed was used to exchange the files, supposedly an FTP† server with the breached organization's domain name (ftp.<Victim Company>.com), was not one that we actually had in our environment.

Something was obviously wrong, but we could not tell what it was. We started the work of filling up their hard drive with logs from our actual file exchange server, which was not reliant on FTP to exchange files, and had never resolved to that URL,‡ just in case we were missing something. But we took a long, hard look at those logs, and there was nothing there.

Then one of our team members had the bright idea to ask for a bit more information regarding how they reached the conclusion that we were involved.

"Would you mind showing us?" he asked them. They were happy to share.

---

* Again, go prove you don't have a sister. Get it?

† File Transfer Protocol – a common method for exchanging files.

‡ Universal Resource Locator – that web address you type into your browser to go places, like www.cnn.com.

And in another moment in a career full of such moments, I felt pretty stupid when we received the answer.

What the analysts in Virginia did was this: they saw an IP* address entry in the logs of Victim Company, and reverse DNSed[†] it to a URL. That URL was ftp.<some other company name>.com – let's assign that "some other company name" the moniker "Exfil Company".[‡]

Now they stripped off the "ftp." leader from the URL, and resolved <Exfil Company>.com to another IP. That IP did in fact belong to us (the "Innocent Bystander"); see Figure 1.1.[§]

So they reached the obvious conclusion that we were the culprit.

Except that this conclusion was wrong.

See, Exfil Company was a customer of our company, and had their main website hosted with us. That was why their <Exfil Company>.com web address resolved (or pointed) to an IP address that pointed our way.

However, they also had an FTP server that they hosted themselves, on their own infrastructure, that we had nothing to do with. That server was the one that was involved in the leak. The back and forth DNS naming and IP resolution process had gotten the investigators confused.

Once we pointed out to them this translation error, several things happened.

First of all, they verified what we said. Then I spoke on the phone with the agent from the San Francisco office, and he thanked us profusely. Said that we really helped the investigation, and indeed, once we pointed them in the right direction, they were able to obtain what they needed, and take the next step in the process of going after the bad guys.

---

* Internet Protocol – a numerical internet address that is used by computers to connect to each other.
† That is, they executed a query to translate the web address to an internet address, which they could then associate with the organization to whom that internet address belonged.
‡ Because their systems were ultimately used as the exfiltration point for the data that was stolen from Victim Company.
§ This is pretty much the extent of my graphic design skills. It took me two hours to do. Your pity is appreciated.

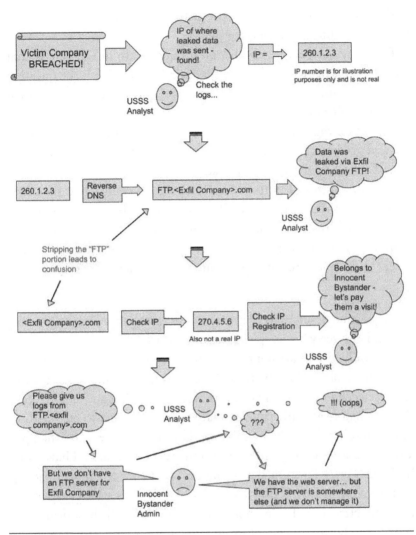

Figure 1.1 A sort-of-visual "flow diagram" of the story.

Both I and the team member who sought clarification were asked to be on standby in case they wanted to summon us as witnesses in the subsequent court case.

And that hard drive they gave us?

They never picked it up. We asked them several times what to do with it, never got a straight answer, and I think legal counsel at the company felt that it was better to let it sit than destroy it ourselves, what with it technically being government property.

For all I know, it may still be sitting in a drawer somewhere in Northern California, collecting dust.

From my perspective, the happiest outcome from this tale is that the fellow on the team who had the brilliant idea to ask the question of the Feds ultimately decided to join forces with EAmmune, my own company. Oh, and it gave me a cool story to share with you, one which illustrates for the umpteenth time just how easy it is to screw up forensics and go down the wrong path, chasing ghosts. Hackers know this too, of course, and use it to their advantage.

A common thread in these two stories is, of course, that for-profit hacking is not imaginary. We all know and fear this, and as much as I can say in retrospect that I have learned from and even enjoyed (in a professional sense) dealing with these and other situations in my career so far, they are never pleasant in the moment that they unfold.

***

Yet a question deserves to be asked: do we fear them a little too much?

Oh, I can see your temples starting to throb.

Certainly if steps are not taken to build in that resilience, leading to the damage being done by these nefarious actors being much greater than it needed to be, then no fear is big enough. Ask any organization that has had to actually pay out a large fee to a hacker to release their critical resources after being sabotaged by ransomware – and then pay a king's ransom on top of that to do the work they should have done in the first place for a much more modest fee to create a proper backup and recovery infrastructure. To put it bluntly, it is a lot cheaper and more effective to make decisions and negotiate for the best deal when your entire business is not at imminent risk of utter destruction.

In fact – and as I write this, I realize that this must be considered testament to some sort of romantic naivete I must still possess about human behavior – it never ceases to amaze me that organizations will spend mucho bucks on security tools, yet somehow not seem to want to consider fundamental basics in security design.

For example: it costs very little to think through where critical data should really, absolutely reside – and then ensure that it never resides anywhere else. You see this problem a lot in the SaaS (and PaaS)*

---

* Software as a Service, and Platform as a Service. Cloud companies, basically.

world, where enterprises will insist that their cloud vendors undergo excruciating security reviews, even in situations where the enterprise can simply choose to interact with the cloud environment only with the exact, non-sensitive information necessary to facilitate the service, and no more. I have heard far more than once the statement, from enterprise business and technology managers, telling a vendor that they "don't trust their own people not to send the wrong data over".

Say what?*

Of course, the SaaS and PaaS vendors really have no choice, so they agree to things they should not because they need the customers, and the customers pat themselves on the back on a job well done – which is true until the vendor does get breached and overwhelmed with the aggregate total of claims for damages and, in the worst case, has to shut its doors. And who suffers in the end? The very enterprise customer whose sensitive data was stolen, data that should *never have been there to be stolen in the first place.*

Quite literally the most fundamental rule in the entire realm of data protection, rule zero, the prime, the essential ingredient, the one rule to rule them all – and by a fair margin – is this simple: *sensitive data should never be stored where it is not absolutely needed to be stored.*

But bad stuff still happens. And between corporate lawyers, PR firms, journalists who understand little about the topics they cover but love to chase the sensational, and an even less informed public, a fascinating dynamic emerges that can shake your faith in fairness and what is right and wrong.

Needless to say, if you are in Security, that faith would have necessarily already been discarded in your first couple of years on the job.

***

A few years back, one of our customers, a retail organization, suddenly developed an interesting case of the leakies. The credit card associations reached out to them with those dreaded internal Common Point of Purchase (CPP) reports that outline what appears to be fraudulent transactions.

---

* Honestly, the people you cannot trust in this case should probably not be managing that kind of data in the first place.

This, dear reader, is a well established "Houston, we have a problem" kind of moment in retail.

We investigated the issue internally. If you have ever had the fortune to be involved in a situation like this, you will have a sense of how it works in real life. It generally goes along the lines of everybody screaming all at once "plans? What plans? We don't have time for plans! Fix it now!", while running around in every possible direction, launching competing theories and just as rapidly discarding them, chasing ghosts and their mirror images, and just acting, acting, *acting*, as panic sets in.

None of that actually helps in dealing with the core issue, but it seems to make people feel better, so I suppose it carries some emotional benefit.

Thankfully, having had rather significant historical experience in matters like this before, we were able to serve as the cool voice in the room. It was time to ask some questions.

"Can we find out whether there is a common pattern?" was, of course, the first one. Specifically, we wanted to find out if the fraudulent transactions were coming from the stores, the call center, or the e-commerce environment, or any combination thereof.

Here, for this organization, there was a complicating factor. We could rule out the call center pretty quickly, but the way they were set up had some legacy components that effectively created a scenario where the e-commerce and store channels would commingle transaction sources to some degree.

It certainly seemed like the website was the biggest offender, but because of this legacy reporting issue, we could not rule out the store environment immediately, and so performed fairly extensive internal forensics on the key systems there. My gut said it was the website, but my gut had failed me before.

Even so, the biggest challenge to overcome was entirely psychological: this organization had suffered in the past a compromise at their store point-of-sale systems – that breach was, in fact, the precipitating event to us working with them to help them flesh out their Security program – and so there was a strong (and painful) sense of deja vu internally.

As a side note, you really *really* do not want to be the guy who was brought in to make sure something never happens again, only to be

looked at by the same people who brought you in with that look saying the obvious, that is, that they are clearing thinking "oh, I can't
effing believe it's happening again".

Trust me on this.

It would be better to be standing in a police lineup.

Ultimately, though, we were able to prove to everybody's satisfaction that the store environment was not the culprit.

It had to be the website.

The problem?

This organization had completely outsourced their e-commerce
operations to an outside SaaS vendor, who provided a turnkey service
for managing the site. In other words, the company – our customer –
had no control over the website, or insight on how it was being run,
except via the vendor's annual PCI attestation of, and report on, compliance (AoC and RoC) provided by the vendor's PCI auditor.

Furthermore, as the internal investigation was unfolding, we discovered a curious pattern; the fraudulent transactions would take
place over a period of time, then stop. Then they would start again,
and then stop. Again and again, this odd behavior would show itself.
That was definitely not normal in the world of for-profit hacking; generally speaking, the bad guys want to get their hands on as much as
possible as quickly as possible while remaining undetected so as to
maximize their return on investment. They might throttle the leak to
avoid detection, but a start and stop approach is atypical.

What, you think hackers do not think in terms of cost, effort, and
income? Of course they do. And they operate under the assumption
that they will eventually get discovered, so they use the time window
between gaining successful entry into the environment to their detection by the organization to steal as much as they can get their paws on.

Why do you think the best ransomware goes after critical network
resources first? Especially network-connected backups and domain
controllers? What better way to truly put your target under the proverbial gun than to cripple their ability to recover from the disabling
event?

But back to our customer. Something strange was clearly afoot, and
we decided to investigate some more while attempting to reach out to
the SaaS vendor to obtain further insights.

As is often, and sadly, the case, the vendor in turn stonewalled our company for as long as they could, refusing to provide audit trails or logs even though they were obligated to do so in the contract, and generally just behaved in the "who, me?" kind of manner you can readily observe with small children caught with their hand in the cookie jar.

Still, this gave us the opportunity to try and figure out what was going on, and ultimately, we found out what it was; the vendor had apparently started adding third party components to the e-commerce sites it was managing to increase referrals and conversions – needless to say, they did it without explicitly seeking permission for each addon from the brands themselves. One of those components* was the culprit, effectively manifesting a cross site request forgery (CSRF, a type of vulnerability) exposure of which a group of hackers had taken advantage to steal credit card information from the consumers who happened to be shopping when the bad application plug-in was being served. The hack actually took place at that third (fourth?) party – it made all the news for a little while – but the end result was a hit for our company (and quite a few others as well).

And the reason for the odd timing pattern? We figured that out too. Early on in the investigation, as a safety measure, we asked the e-commerce provider to roll back the site to its prior known good state – that is, effectively before the suspected fraud began – which they did. But it turns out that the application plug-in component had a "call home" feature that would allow it to update itself every couple of weeks to the newest iteration. So the site would be restored with an older, clean version of the plug-in, and then at some undetermined point after that restoration point, it would update itself to the vulnerable version ... thereby alerting the hackers behind the exploit that they could start stealing data again. The fraud would subsequently resume on all the sites that included that newly updated version of the plug-in.

Welcome to the world of security, where everything is transient, and your migraines only grow, and never subside.

I would like to note at this point the remarkable complexity of this chain: our customer was not directly attacked. Neither was

---

* Called an "iFrame".

their website, which was managed by a third party. What caused the breach was poor operational practices at that third party – specifically, failing to perform proper validation of external code being hosted on their platform – which allowed hackers at *their* third party (in effect our customer's fourth party) to steal data from our customer's customers' browsers via a specific variation of a man-in-the-middle attack.

How's your headache?

Anyway, once we figured all of this out, we instructed the vendor to remove all third party plug-ins and handed the whole affair off to the lawyers. We also informed the credit card associations, providing them with all the evidence to prove that it was not our brand that was directly at fault, which mostly got them off our backs. In fact, not only did they not pursue any action against the brand, they actually thanked us and asked us if we could be on standby if they needed more evidence that they could pursue with the e-commerce vendor. We further provided the evidence to a couple of attorneys general who had reached out because of state privacy laws.

Then we sat back to watch the fireworks.

***

So here's a question for ya: what do you think actually happened next? Let me sharpen my query a little. What do you think happened to the e-commerce vendor?

After all, while the exploit was not in their own code, its manifestation on their platform, which resulted in tens of millions of compromised credit card accounts across multiple brands, was entirely their fault. They did two things wrong: (1) they failed to perform a security review of the third-party plug-in they hosted inside their platform; and (2) they added that plug-in without asking their customer brands whether they would want them installed.

We had incontrovertible, undeniable proof of these claims. Our evidence was strong enough to get VISA and Mastercard, as well as two Attorneys General, to agree that our side was simply a victim, and they used this information to trace it back to at least a dozen more brands impacted by the same issue.

So, what happened to the SaaS vendor?

Did they have to notify the media?

Were they forced to shell out large sums of money for damages incurred by their combined customer base that was negatively impacted?

Were there any class actions? Any other lawsuits?

Did they lose any customers?

What do you think happened?

I'll give you a minute.

Ready?

In one word, this is what happened:

Nothing.

Nothing happened.

The media never caught wind of it – in fact, to this day, there is not a single media story about that event which explicitly mentions the e-commerce vendor. Not one. There are plenty of stories about their customers, the brands whose websites got hacked, but the vendor's name somehow never made it into any one of them.

To the best of my knowledge, not a single lawsuit was ever filed. The lawyers for both parties negotiated some settlements behind the scenes, which if our customer is an example of, amounted to the vendor paying out for the internal investigation costs and part of the costs for notifying consumers, while not admitting fault. In aggregate, it is clear that the amounts ultimately did not cross the threshold of their overall cyberliability insurance umbrella.

For all I can tell, they did not lose a single customer, even amongst those who were breached.

I can imagine that this vendor's cyber insurance premiums went up after the event to some degree, but in the end, it became a big, fat nothingburger.

When I asked our customer why they chose not to pursue this more aggressively – after all, we had plenty of proper (and with chain of evidence intact) proof to do so – they told us that honestly, they just wanted to move on from this affair. When we asked why they didn't at least look to switch providers, they admitted that doing so would be a big pain in the neck, and so they felt that with the issue resolved, it was easier to just stick around with the vendor, and hope that they would have learned from their mistake.

In other words, avoiding the potential for further embarrassment that the publicity of a lawsuit would bring, combined with platform lock-in, led our largely online based retailer to the conclusion that "it wasn't so bad after all".

The fear of negative PR kept our customer at bay.

The SaaS vendor continued to operate normally and without even having to promise to improve.

And if this doesn't depress you about the field of Infosec, nothing will.

***

In reality, though, this isn't actually very surprising, seeing how people prefer not to think about security in general.

And it also leads us naturally into the next chapter, where the first story I will be sharing is the kind of security and legal horror movie that could give your nightmares a good run for their money.

If you are into this sort of thing, anyway.

2
LIE-ABILITY

When the intersection of Infosec and the legal discipline comes into view, it always appears as a sort of complex concrete beast, like my home town Oakland's MacArthur Maze, or Birmingham's Spaghetti Junction.* It goes in all directions at once, has many layers, and you can never quite tell where each part begins or ends when looking at it from above, but one thing is clear: they are clearly intertwined.

There are many reasons for this being a reflection of Security+Legal, but I put it down to two primary drivers.

First, the discipline of Infosec is very much a sibling of Legal. In my view, the essential function of general counsel in a corporate setting is to protect the company from legal and commercial liability. Crudely stated, we can sum it up as "let's make sure we don't cross any lines that would create too much exposure for the business to sustain, and while we're at it, let's try to keep everyone away from the orange jumpsuits".

In this context, Security serves as a sort of third arm, in that it primarily deals with protecting the company from technology liability. For a while, this last bit also included data liability, but now that data privacy (or simply "Privacy") is becoming its own thing, the fundamentals are shifting ever so slightly. It also, incidentally, tells you that the Chief Privacy Officer – or CPO – is set to become just as important as the Chief Information Security Officer (CISO) in coming years, and that they must become independent functions.†

Speaking as someone who had previously held both titles simultaneously in well known, fairly large organizations, that comes as a big relief.

---

* Turns out that there are many other similarly named spaghetti junctions, but I first heard the term in Birmingham (the one in the UK), so I am going with that one.
† So that is definitely something GDPR got right.

DOI: 10.1201/9781003133308-3   **37**

The second driver, and the one that truly complicates everything, is that the practitioners from either side – Security and Legal – do not always seem to want to recognize the need for cooperation between the two disciplines.

The blame falls equally on both parties, each of whom is naturally very protective of their domains. Counsel knows, with absolute certainty, that the intricacies of contract law are too much for the layperson. The CISO likewise knows, with the same level of certainty, that the same principle applies in security operations.

And yet, as the world shifts faster and faster into technology reliance, abstractions, data sharing, and fuzzy technology and data boundaries, the legal and information security disciplines must cooperate and collaborate evermore. Often, the sides are not well prepared to engage with each other, and the end result is a litany of terrible practices that unnecessarily complicate commercial transactions while at the same time reducing the usefulness of the relevant articles. Consequently, this increases the liability gray areas.

You know, the thing everyone set out to reduce in the first place.

I know I promised you a book of stories, and I am about to deliver in this realm as well, but this topic is so critical that I hope you will forgive me this small indulgence, as I spend another couple of pages describing the worst of these bad practices.

Specifically, I want to address the issue of incorporating prescriptive security controls in contracts with vendors. This is where a company tells their vendors that they must configure their password policies just so, or use a specific encryption algorithm, or abide with an explicit set of patching timelines, or any number of similarly inane requirements.

Why are they inane?

Because of two reasons: one, no vendor can manage their internal security controls off of contractual commitments with hundreds or thousands of customers – especially not when they inevitably start conflicting with each other (and they do, because their customers run different security programs); and two, security standards themselves evolve constantly and what might be good today will not be good tomorrow. Contracts, on the other hand, are signed once and generally left to live peacefully ever after.

How many outstanding contracts out there state something like "vendor shall set passwords to be at least seven characters long"? They state it because for quite a while, that is what the payment card industry (PCI) said, and when counsel asked the CISO what they should use, they told them "use that" (with an unspoken "and get out of my face" addendum), and everyone congratulated themselves on work well done, and got on with their lives.

The task was completed. It did not need to be revisited.

But even PCI has advanced since then, and suggests that the appropriate password controls should follow the guidelines in the current revision of NIST 800-63. In other words, the PCI standard itself acknowledges that another, more fundamental standard from the National Institute of Standards and Technology (NIST) might evolve faster, and encapsulates this more advanced standard within itself by reference.

Similarly, there are numerous outstanding, live contracts out there that state that a vendor must use "at least" SSL 3 (or TLS 1.0, or even SSL 2!) for encryption in transit. Except all of those protocols have now been broken.* Yet the old contracts are still there, and they still state an insecure level of encryption, because very few of us actually go back and update contracts when security standards evolve. It is not that easy to do, especially since it requires both parties to effectively renegotiate, and why should anyone be motivated to do so if they are otherwise happy with the arrangement? That would be an enormous waste of effort.

And if you think a security leader can force their own company to terminate an existing and successful business relationship with a critical vendor just because they insist that some obscure technical contractual clause must be changed ... well ... to quote oh so many, I would like some of what you're smoking. Even on the rare occasion where that security leader might succeed (typically, in fear-based cultures), they will lose a tremendous amount of political capital in the process.

---

* Meaning they are no longer secure, and should not be used for sensitive data exchanges.

Yet, to stick to the same example, if you look at PCI, it has itself evolved, and very clearly no longer allows the use of these older protocols.

See how that works? Why not do the same in contracts? Just state that password controls and minimum encryption standards must conform to the guidelines in the current version of the NIST 800 series, or the prevailing version of PCI, and trust that the folks publishing those standards will continue to evolve them – at which point the evolution of those standards is *automatically incorporated into the contract without it ever needing to be changed!*

It brings contracts in line with the reality of Security and keeps them that way in the long term, which both smooths out the process of negotiations and increases security for both sides for the entire life of the contract, not just the moment of signing the bottom line.

Don't even get me started about the utter pointless insanity of security questionnaires.

***

(Horror) story time.

We were sitting in the offices of our Fortune 500 customer in Silicon Valley, and discussing a number of issues related to their upcoming (massive and complex) PCI audit, when the door opened.

The lead developer of their new mobile applications division walked in. We will call him Mike.

"We have a design meeting right after lunch", he says. "Would you mind joining us? I want to make sure we don't miss anything important".

As a side note, that we had managed to instill this culture in the engineering organization of such a large company should not be taken lightly. That we had managed to do that way back at the time this took place is still a point of pride for me.

We were obviously delighted to participate.

To set the context for what followed, I will share with you that this was roughly around the time that these new privacy regulations in Europe were still in early discussion. In fact, the General Data Protection Regulation (GDPR) moniker was not yet in existence, and the EU privacy commission was not even fully assembled, but at the same time, the gist of what will ultimately become the rules was clearly taking shape: the EU was serious about this, they were going after the big players (one of whom was our customer, a large business-to-consumer multinational), and they meant for it to have actual teeth.

And if you listened at all, you could infer quite easily that they wanted to give consumers as much control over their personal data as possible.

So we went into the meeting, which lasted all afternoon, and gave our feedback and suggestions to each part of the design. This is incidentally one of my favorite roles to play – today, when I am asked to join an advisory board for a security product company, I am typically far more interested in being on the "technology advisory" team, wherein I get to influence product direction, rather than serve primarily in the typical advisory role as a sort of awkward extension of the business development team. It feels like a position with much more impact for me to occupy.

Towards the end of the meeting we got our chance to suggest new elements that the product team might wish to consider, and we brought up the obvious one: privacy.

This was to be a mobile application with a very large anticipated install base and users all over the world, including in the EU. It would accumulate a lot of consumer Personally Identifiable Information (PII), and it was clear to the product team that the application infrastructure, and especially the technology infrastructure back end, needed to incorporate some features to protect that PII. We had already answered some questions in this regard earlier in the meeting.

One thing that had not yet been discussed was how to handle the use case where a user might reach out to the company and ask for their personal data to be deleted. The term Data Subject Access Rights (DSAR) Request had not come into existence quite yet, but the concept was already percolating heavily and everyone knew it would become part of those eventual privacy rules. We wanted to make sure that the product team built some controls into the product that would support the capability of addressing these kinds of requests in an automated fashion.

Our suggestion was to build what we called a "big red button" library. What this library would do was, upon receipt of a user ID, engage with all data repositories in the organization and methodically remove all data associated with that user ID, while producing a log of this activity. This way, whenever a request for deletion would come through, the application could call the library (or push the big red button) and nuke that person's details out of existence, in an auditable fashion.

Mike was ecstatic.

"This is great!" he said, "and we could also use it for other things, like data retrieval for a profile". Of course, ultimately this also became a right encapsulated within the GDPR, wherein a consumer could request a full record of all the information a company possessed on them, in an easily consumable format.*

He continued. "Now that I think about it, we need to build this concept of a uniform ID everywhere in the supporting infrastructure – since we haven't even started coding it yet, it will be easy, and will make our lives so much easier down the road. This would have been so much harder to do later!"

Well, we certainly agreed with that.

Everyone left the meeting happy.

Mike had a new insight that he felt was useful, would make his life easier, and gave him a whole slew of new ideas on how to make a better product. We felt like we had contributed something of value into the conversation; as a consultant, you are rarely if ever given credit for what you did yesterday, or even an hour ago. That old joke about the consultant asking for your watch to tell you the time is, indeed, very … very … old.

We had a couple of quick follow-up conversations with Mike over the rest of the week, but overall everything seemed to be on track. Our input allowed him to avoid some potentially costly design errors, especially in view of the upcoming privacy regulations, which he had no idea about when we started talking. We knew it would make our jobs easier down the road once the regulations were finalized. And our sponsoring executive in the company seemed delighted that he had an opportunity to showcase our positive contributions to his colleagues.

***

Three weeks later, Mike came to see us again.

---

* AKA the "right of data portability".

As I am writing this, I realize that what transpired next is just as astonishing and shocking today as it was back then. Not just because of the particulars of the story, but also because of the sort of sadly common thinking that eventually led to the manifestation of what can fairly be described as an especially perverted end result.

Mike, in a resigned tone, began by telling us that they had decided to move on without the "big red button library". As we expressed equal elements of surprise and confusion, especially in light of his prior enthusiasm about the idea, he reiterated his complete agreement that the concept felt right, and that at this stage, it would be easy to implement.

"But," he continued, "I have no choice. Legal told me not to do it".

It took us a few seconds to gather our collective jaws off the floor where they fell, and one of us finally mustered the necessary control over their vocal cords to ask the obvious question:

"What? But why?!"

Mike went on to explain.

He said that as they were putting together the final design, he got a call from general counsel. Let us call that guy Robin. I wish to remind you at this time that Robin was general counsel at a Fortune 500 firm, a massive multinational with an immense volume of consumer data that was only set to grow exponentially.

Mike told us that Robin instructed him, in no uncertain terms, to absolutely and under no circumstances, ever build this sort of facility into that product or any other that the company was designing and building.

Furthermore, Mike added, Robin told him to change the design such that it would make it as difficult as possible to ever be able to reconstruct a full set of "knowledge" the company might have about any single consumer. So hard, in fact, that it would be practically impossible to do so without great effort and expense.

We politely inquired if Mike knew what the thinking was behind this approach. We didn't expect that he would, but we had to ask. He admitted that he did not, but he had to follow these instructions, even though it would actually and needlessly complicate the design of his product as well as others (not to mention the associated demoralizing effect of asking a top engineer to intentionally build things less efficiently). With that, at least, we could concur.

But what on earth could possibly justify the directive he was given?

We knew that Robin's team, who were (as you would expect) both very large and deeply experienced, knew about the upcoming privacy regulations. Was it some sort of misunderstanding? We asked Mike to give us 48 hours to try and figure it out.

Then we reached out for clarification through our corporate sponsor.

When it comes right down to it, the line of thinking that came back (on the phone, in what was clearly a somewhat irritated tone) made a perfect kind of twisted sense.

Robin first learned of the idea after our sponsor, who viewed it as a win, reported on it enthusiastically in one of the senior executive forums.

And he did not like it one little bit.

The way Legal viewed the issue was that the rules were not actually in place yet, but between their internal and external teams they knew quite a bit about what they were going to look like. Their prediction* was that in the ultimate version, the rules will have an escape hatch of sorts.

Specifically, they were fairly certain that any company could avoid having to comply with the privacy rules that were to become the GDPR by arguing and successfully showing at trial – if it ever got that far – that it could not reasonably implement such compliance without undue burden on their business. That is, that to achieve compliance would require such a massive investment of time and effort that it would endanger the company's very existence, making it practically impossible. Instead, the company would at that point only need to comply to a lesser degree, to a "reasonableness" standard, and (the next part is my conjecture about the unspoken part) get to do what it wants with consumer data. In particular, they could keep as much of it as possible forever, which is what they were wanting to do all along.

In simple terms, their idea was that a company could more or less *ignore GDPR if it could show that it could not effectively comply with it.* From a legal point of view, I suppose that this may have been correct; as a security and privacy leader, I simply could not believe my ears.

Perhaps sadly, I cannot share with you what actually transpired from this decision, as it took a few years for things to play out, well

---

* Which, depressingly enough, turned out to be sort of correct, at least initially.

past the time when our engagement ended. As the company itself underwent dramatic changes and lost a huge slice of market share, it is entirely possible to assume that in the end, it never got to the point where this uniquely crafted legal opinion was ever tested in court.

Still, it serves as a pretty dramatic illustration of the intersection of Legal and Security (and Privacy).

***

This intersection between the two domains of Infosec and Legal is always present, and while it can lead to mind-expanding experiences like that one I just shared, it can also lead to some amusing ones.

As an example that was personally meaningful to me, and in a context that mixes in an element of law enforcement as well as a sprinkling of diplomacy, let us go back all the way to the early Oughts, when I was still trying to get my consulting business off the ground. Part of doing that involved getting into all sorts of pro bono endeavors in an effort to build a network and possibly identify some opportunities for paid work.

One such project was Think Security First, which came about in response to President Bush's call for increased cyber security awareness amongst the nation's population. I came to be involved in it after joining the chamber of commerce at Walnut Creek, California. The fellow who was the driving force behind it, and who has since become a dear friend, is also one of the most brilliant minds in the world when it comes to "human security" – Neal O'Farrell. It was a simple concept, but one that was extremely hard to execute successfully: to make an entire medium-sized city increase security awareness across all of its resident population. Just figuring out what "success" meant was challenging. Ultimately, when all was said and done, I think it did pretty well, and even got some brief attention from national news media, including coverage on CNN. From my own perspective, it also ended up leading to a couple of paid gigs, and my first couple of security-related TV media appearances.

But Think Security First is not the reason behind this story, but that's where I met Neal, who is actually the reason.

A couple of years later, Neal called me up and asked if I would be willing to join him and a colleague of his on a "day trip" (his words, not mine) to the offices of the State Department in San Francisco.

"Sure", I responded, maybe a bit too hastily. Even without knowing what this was about, it sounded like it would be fun. Neal, a student of human behavior, laughed (at me) and then proceeded to explain. This was to be a round table discussion with some eastern European government officials about the topic of global cyber crime, something in which the Bush administration had taken a significant interest. Neal thought* that recommending to State to add me to the mix would reflect well, and make this into a bigger success.

To cut a long story short, there was "some" paperwork to fill, and some agreements to sign, and then on the appointed Tuesday we arrived at the federal building bright and early (read: 8:30 AM, which in nerdland is practically dead of night). I met Neal's colleague, who was clearly the smartest guy in the room, and also ultimately became a friend, Lance James.[†] We were given very formal looking badges, shown in to the conference room, and met the rest of the crew, including the eastern Europeans. I took an immediate liking to those guys; one of them, a high-ranking officer of internal police, even gave me a standing invitation to come visit them in Sofia and enjoy his wife's Banitsa.[‡] Another fellow, who apparently held the "rank equivalent" of colonel and an impressive title within the ministry of the interior, told us later that he used to be a Soviet intelligence officer assigned to the Sofia desk (read: former spy), which apparently did not bother anyone.[§]

While the meeting itself was fascinating to me, and I even managed to make a couple of useful contributions (or so I like to think), the reason I tell you this story is tangential to the meeting. It is, however, also what illustrates again these domain intersections and makes it so funny.

---

* Naively, obviously.

† Many years later, Lance wrote the foreword to *Why CISOs Fail*.

‡ This is a great example of how meaningless cultural trivia tidbits can suddenly become useful; having grown up in Israel, where Bourekas is the national pastry, I happened to be quite familiar with the Bulgarian version, and mentioned it early on as a way to make conversation. I did not expect it to have such an impact!

§ I never had any inclination to validate the veracity of this claim. I just found it fascinating that he dropped it so casually, and it stuck in my mind.

As we neared the top of the eleventh hour,* we took a small break, and the lady from State with whom I had been communicating in the weeks leading to the meeting and who had met us when we arrived, cracked open the door.

"Mr. Engel", she murmured. I turned to her and she motioned for me to step out. I promptly got out of my chair and headed outside. We went around the corner.

She raised her eyes to me, a concerned look on her face.

"Mr. Engel", she started (I tried telling people there to just call me "Barak" but it didn't work, so I had given up by that point), "I really hate to ask you this, and I don't mean to offend you".

I raised my eyebrows. I was having a grand ol' time. What on earth could she possibly say to offend me?

"Well …" she hesitated, "I'm not entirely sure how to ask this but …"

I waited.

"Are you an American citizen?" she finally blurted out.

"No", I said, "I have my application in and it should be approved in a few months, but it hasn't happened yet".

Her face turned a shade paler.

It took me a couple of seconds, and then it dawned on me.

Here I was, casually representing the private sector in an event sponsored by the United States of America's State Department, in a sort of informal gathering with foreign government officials … in what was essentially an international forum on cyber crime … and I wasn't even a US citizen.

While probably not a breach of any regulations, it certainly seemed like a potential impropriety, or at the very least, not according to protocol.

The postscript to this story that helped reinforce this hunch came a few days later. I was having an unrelated conversation with an agent in the local FBI office with whom I had become acquainted due to another matter, and after we were done chatting about our topic, he mentioned that they got an unusual request earlier in the week to "urgently" wrap up my citizenship background check. He suggested

---

* This *extremely clever* wordplay is meant to indicate a time of around 10:55 AM. Nothing more. I promise.

that they did not usually see those and was wondering what led to it. I shared the story with him, and he laughed and added, "that probably explains it".

As it happens, I ended up becoming a proud new citizen in what appeared to be slightly ahead of schedule.

***

Infosec in the private sector does, of course, often have a direct footprint within the legal realm via its undeniable connection with law enforcement. Or at least it should; I find myself constantly taken aback by how so many technical security leaders seem to treat this crucial aspect of their job responsibility as no more than an unpleasant afterthought. That is, if they do not simply ignore it completely.

I suppose it is possible that I have just been more unlucky than most.*

The advantage of decades of such rotten luck is that I had developed an unusual and perhaps unfortunate instinct about where the wrong thing might be going on.

This ultimately leads to a, uhh, finely honed sense of cynicism.

For example, when I build the security posture for cloud platform (PaaS) companies, I will always be extremely vigilant in ensuring that they stay away from any human handling of customer data, other than when the product itself does so programmatically according to their customers' instructions. Human involvement is generally verboten, unless the customer explicitly asks for support, and then only for that purpose. This approach, which ends up infusing the companies' master services agreement and set of commercial obligations, is in my opinion the only reasonable one in a legal and commercial sense, as it maintains a clear demarcation between the platform, which acts as a sandbox, and the customer using it and their data (which under this concept stays as much as possible under their control). Otherwise the boundaries get super fuzzy super quick and while it can keep the lawyers fed, it similarly keeps security and especially privacy practitioners from getting any sleep.

I like sleep.

---

* Then again, I have been building or guiding security departments in dozens of organizations, perhaps even more than a hundred (I haven't really counted), so maybe it is simply a matter of the law of *fairly large* numbers.

All of this makes sense, but it does create a problem when I try to explain it to someone who has never had to think about it before.

A few years back, I was working with the new general counsel at one of our customer PaaS companies, and since it is always a top priority for me, I brought up this topic early on. I also tied it to why I wanted to invite an agent from the local FBI office of computer crimes over, to get the relationship going with them. That made counsel uncomfortable – law enforcement was something they preferred to avoid. As I was trying to explain the reasoning behind my line of thinking, they asked me for an example.

"Sure", I said, and took a long breath as my brain was frantically running through the gears to come up with a relatable answer that made contextual sense for this particular company. "Here's one: anyone can sign up for the free version of the service, right?"

"Yes", they replied.

"OK. And we don't actually monitor what they do, because that would create all sorts of liability that we would like to avoid – it's better if we don't look into their data payloads. With me so far?"

"Right. Gotcha", came the response, and then after a second of hesitation, "makes sense; we don't want to touch their data or even know what's in it, because then we end up owning the data liability in addition to the platform liability".

"Exactly", I said. "But what it also means is that anyone can sign up for the free service and use the platform to do things that they shouldn't do, legally. Right?"

"Hold on, no, that doesn't sound right. They would be violating our terms and conditions if they did that", they responded.

"Sure, assuming our T&Cs were properly crafted – which I'm sure they are", I added hastily, narrowly avoiding an infection with the proverbial foot in mouth disease.

"But this still doesn't stop someone from actually doing the wrong thing anyway. Just like the law doesn't stop people from committing crimes. They still do, and then we hope to catch them and punish them via law enforcement".

"Right", they said, "we all get that. So ... about that example?" To their credit, this particular counsel was an unusually patient one.

"Getting to it", I smiled. "So let's take a hypothetical: someone opens up a free account and then uses it to process, exchange, and even facilitate illegal gambling ... we wouldn't even know it was happening, because we don't look at their data. That's why it's so essential that we establish a relationship with law enforcement up front, so when the subpoena comes, we can deal with it in a more, shall I say, friendly fashion. Makes sense?"

"Completely. Thank you", they said.

I got the FBI relationship going, and we moved on.

***

A few weeks later, counsel calls me.

"Barak, I have to say, your gambling example really stuck in my mind", they tell me.

"Great", I fire back, "glad it felt useful".

"No, you don't understand at all. Can we chat privately?"

So I went to their office.

Turns out that they had just received a subpoena from a different FBI office across the country ... related to a free account on our platform ... that was apparently using it as part of an illegal online gambling operation.

Due to the established relationship, we were able to quickly reach out to our local FBI field office and rapidly transition the interaction with the Feds into a much smoother (dare I say friendlier?) one than counsel ever expected.

For their part, counsel was grateful, a bit in awe, and also (they admitted) a bit suspicious. As for me, I do not know about you and how you would react, but from my perspective, that was one of the best "*told you so! LOL*" moments I had ever experienced.

***

I got to experience a similar, even more satisfying moment, in a different interaction with a three-letter agency.

As part of a long-standing relationship, and based on a certain report that I had made many years before, I was occasionally asked for any ideas I might be able to share with them with respect to possible "infrastructure level" attack vectors they should consider.

There are all sorts of forums for encouraging public-private collaborations intended to facilitate these kinds of communications. A well known and respected one is Infragard, in which I am proud to hold a membership. But this particular interaction did not come from one of those; instead, it was an agent – let's call him Holvis – who had taken an interest in my views of the industry and thought that I had a knack for coming up with fresh ideas.

Plus, if something I suggested to him panned out, that would look good on his resume, too.

The problem was – still is – that I tend to be very careful in making any sort of prediction, unless I am fairly convinced that it is worth chasing. Our conversations typically took the form of him telling me in a slightly frustrated tone to "just tell me what you see, even if it's wild", to which I would respond with "oh, nothing you probably haven't already seen yourselves".

It is fair to say that I can sometimes be exasperating to deal with.

On this occasion, though, I did think of something that I thought was interesting. It was still pretty wild to me, but just enough on this side of crazy that I shared it. It took about 30 minutes to lay out the theory, explain how it all works, and why I thought it might be an area that they would want to look into at a national scale. The more I explained, the more crazy I sounded to myself, but Holvis was extremely interested. He wrote down pages of notes, and asked me what seemed like a million questions to make sure he understood the technical aspects of this half baked idea I had just shared with him about where a next big attack could come from.

Then the conversation ended, our coffee mugs were empty, and we parted ways.

I promptly forgot about it.

***

Maybe six months later, we had another meeting. We go through the usual conversations, and then he says, "do you have something new for me?"

"What do you mean?" I say.

"You know. One of those crazy ideas", he says, a smile at the corner of his mouth.

"Not really", I respond, "and why are you smiling like that?"

He goes on to tell me that he had compiled a report on that "thing" we talked about that other time – he had to remind me what it was – and submitted it to headquarters. Then, not even two months later, a big attack was launched on the very same point in the infra-structure that I had pointed out to him, and in exactly the fashion I had proposed.

No one else had brought it up to them before he did it with his report, and the correlated timing made it seem borderline prophetic. As you might imagine, it made the rounds (and apparently made him look really good for having me as a source).

The positive part of all this is that I felt the warm glow of having contributed something useful at that scale, and the powerful sense of personal validation that comes from erroneously ascribing dumb luck to one's own cleverness.

You know, another one of them *"told you so! LOL"* moments.

The bad part was that now they expected me to come up with another one.

***

Working domestically with three-letter agencies is one thing, but once you go global, jurisdictional issues can become the kind of PITA* in which one does not want to have their falafel.

Back when I was still a pup in Israel, learning the network engi-neering trade, I got exposed to such jurisdictional issues for the first time. If you are old enough to recall one of the big early hackery (ha) news items from the Nineties, you might remember the story of the Analyzer. He was a hacker who broke into all sorts of sensitive US government systems, including the Pentagon's, and it made some major headlines back in the day.

Well, turns out he was a kid in Herzliya, in Israel, and the way we knew this before the public did was that the FBI, CIA, National Security Agency (NSA), and some others reached out to my employer, an ISP,† to talk to us about it. The fellow they talked to on our end and who really took the lead on supporting their efforts, by the name of Steve Birnbaum, is someone I am proud to call friend to this day, and you might run into him if you hang around DC long enough,

---

* If you're unfamiliar with the acronym, look it up. My "bad word allocation" is at a frightening deficit.
† Internet Service Provider. It was called Netvision, and at the time, was dominant in the Israeli market (and big even by European standards). I was serving as the com-pany's network architect at the time, so I was involved by definition.

especially around Federal Emergency Management Agency (FEMA) peeps. Count yourself lucky if you do.

Now, I want to be clear about what I mean when I say "they reached out to us", because while I assume there was some of that at the beginning, I was not exposed to it then, and by the time that I was involved, I do not mean they reached out to us by phone.

Oh no.

By the time Steve pulled me in to talk to me about it, they had sent a government (military?) plane full of agents from these various agencies, and said group came to our offices. So you might say I was somewhat curious about who these guys in suits were.

Especially seeing as suits and ties were not normal business attire in summery, hot Israel.

Turns out the Analyzer was using our network for his activities, and so I ended up participating in the effort to locate him by digging into forensic logs and helping discover his actual identity. Nothing much, really; I was a bit player, even if in all fairness every person involved contributed something essential to the investigation. Steve himself actually ended up in court in the US testifying about this incident later on.

And as these kinds of investigations always do, this served as an early (for me) example of the intersecting domains of legal, law enforcement, and security.

As an amusing aside, years later when I was working with the Think Security First crew, I mentioned being involved with the Analyzer capture efforts as maybe a useful thing to mention in my bio. A few weeks later I saw the marketing material that was put out by the team doing that, and I guess the PR guys got a little overly excited, because they proclaimed that I was "the security guy who caught the famous hacker, the Analyzer!" This was patently untrue, and not what I told them at all. I remember calling Steve in embarrassment to share this with him and to apologize. Still, if you dig hard enough for old local news archives from the early Oughts, you can probably still find those references.*

---

* I assure you, they are wrong. I was involved, but to go from that to I "caught" that guy is a ... uh ... *bit of a stretch.*

On my part, one thing I learned from this incident was how difficult jurisdictional issues can be; it became clear very early on that in some ways, the US government was lucky that this hacker was from Israel, could be extradited, and that due to the special relationship between the countries, they were able to secure the cooperation of Israeli authorities. Were he from, say, one of the former Balkans, it might have been a lot more challenging.

One other example I can share from that time period is a lot sketchier. Before I do, I want to make sure that it is clear that this is not, in any way, to suggest that I condone or support what was going on. Merely that it illustrates how enforcing what seems like common sense rules today may have been a lot trickier back then than one might have expected.

Our ISP was very big (in the local context), and had a lot of very smart people working for it. One of them – call him Barry – was working in systems administration, and was always doing "cool things" on the side. Well, one of those "cool things" turned out to be the creation and hosting of one of the largest Internet porn servers of the era, right in our own data center. I am not sure how many senior leaders of the company knew about it, but at least one did – because he was an avid consumer of the content.

Think of it as an extremely early version of Pornhub, without the streaming (which did not exist back then), but with a well-indexed and easy to search file repository. As much as I hate to say it, this server most likely also had a fairly large selection of child porn, too, which I came to realize because a related inquiry came in from the good ol' US of A at some point about it.

But the reality was that the laws at the time back home did not necessarily preclude this sort of thing. So Barry kept collecting and curating the videos he liked, indexing them for anyone to peruse at their leisure. And because our ISP sized uplinks from Israel were vastly underutilized,* the fact that many people around the world became users for a little while did not actually "cost" the company anything, so it was tolerated.

It actually made the business appear bigger.

---

* This is because Internet consumers tend to consume a lot of bandwidth downstream, to download content, but much less so on the other side, to upload it.

Eventually he did shut it down after too many people started asking questions, and there were indications that some laws were going to be drafted in Israel, too (as part of a larger trend, not because of his ... efforts). Jurisdiction kept the entire endeavor quasi legal, even if it was not particularly, well, wholesome.

It still does in so many cases involving computer crime.

Jurisdiction is maybe the biggest reason as to why you have so many hackers in certain eastern European countries where the laws are less strict. They may be breaking laws in the US, but not at home, and that allows them to proceed while avoiding the risk of prosecution. After all, even hackers value their freedom.

***

Lest you think that my experiences in this area have been limited only to other people doing arguably bad things, it is time for me to dissuade you of this notion. Like many old timers in this field, some of the stuff I had done earlier in my career would be, at best, questionable today. The story I want to share with you here involves what we shall euphemistically term "business intelligence gathering".

Since double negatives are extremely useful in the context of such stories ... it wasn't illegal. In fact, it was strongly encouraged by all parties involved, at least from my (rather naive) perspective.

But looking back with the somewhat more critical eye of a security practitioner with decades of experience, I can safely say that it stunk to high heaven.

Enough teasing. Let's get to it.

The time is smack dab in the middle of the Internet bubble, and my job involved a lot of cool Internet technology elements. As a part of my daily activities, I was deconstructing networking protocols and tweaking their parameters in borderline unacceptable ways,* managing the resulting chaos in our (mostly by necessity) overly complicated

---

* When the ISP that employs you must deal with fiber costs to the US that are in the range of $60,000 per *month* for an E1 (that is, ~2 Mb/s, about what streaming a single video requires), you have to come up with a lot of clever ways to squeeze every last bit of performance from that piping. My knowledge of the unspoken corners of the routing protocols Enhanced Interior Gateway Routing Protocol (EIGRP) and Border Gateway Protocol (BGP) became so deep that it ultimately landed me a job in the US, for a company that recruited me out of Israel largely for this reason. I came, and I stayed.

network infrastructure, writing code to support rapid automated switching of entire routing protocol instruction blocks on the fly as needed for performance, and interacting with the European agency in charge of allocations of Internet addresses, called the Réseaux IP Européens Network Coordination Centre (RIPE NCC), or RIPE for short.

I was also working with the company's business* sales team to help them sign up new accounts, adopting a secondary role as the company's "business SE" (sales engineer, although the term did not actually exist). In this capacity, my exposure through daily interactions to the company's big hitters in sales led to many friendships, and importantly, deep and highly valuable insights into the sales process. You have to understand that we were basically inventing this stuff as we went along; there were no clear models at the time that anyone followed, there was no such job as an SE, and these guys basically figured it out for themselves. The first salesperson in this team actually started as a customer support person in the days when all of our customers were individuals who desired a dial-up (modem) based Internet connection at home.

We therefore knew each other well, and he started asking for help with those big sales, and it became a thing that we did together.

Anyway, while in the earlier days the company faced a mostly green field, you can bet your life that this changed quickly, and by the time this story happened, there were a couple of aggressive competitors working hard to grab market share. The biggest of them really had our number, and managed to repeatedly grab deals that our folks thought should be ours.

One day I was having lunch with two of these enterprise guys, and they were bitching about this issue, which I very much enjoyed as I was learning a lot from their conversation. Then one of them, whom we shall name David, turned to me and said "Hey, Barak, maybe you can help us. Can you find a way to tell us which deals they are about to close?"

I looked at him in surprise. "How do you mean?" I asked.

"You know. Break into their systems or something. You're the smart one", David said.

---

* Enterprise, in modern parlance.

"Come on, you know I can't do that", I answered.

"What do you mean, you can't? I know you can", he said, in reference to his (admittedly fair) assessment of my technical security skills at the time.

"Sure, but that doesn't seem right", I said.

"Well, is there anything you can do?"

***

Turns out there was.

That conversation ended up percolating in my mind for a few days. Somewhat providentially, I was also working during that time to build some automation for interacting with RIPE to preregister Internet address (IP) spaces for our new enterprise customers. It was a small code base, a mere couple of thousands of lines long, but even at that size it was pretty complex and required a solid chunk of hours to debug properly before we started using it.

After all, nobody wanted to mess up communications with RIPE. That was our lifeblood. We could not afford to screw things up. In order to do this properly, I had to learn all the ins and outs of how the RIPE systems worked.

I became pretty intimate with all of it.

As I was wrapping up the project, I was running some final debugging steps, when on a whim I decided to see if I could use the tool to grab the details of preregistrations from other companies. Turned out that the way RIPE did things, it was entirely possible, as long as I had a certain identifier that would only be known to the originating organization. If I had it, I could question the RIPE database for the registration details.

Which in the case of any ISP, would include the name of the customer they were registering the IP space for.

To make customers' new connections work as quickly as possible following successful registration, you would want your Internet "address server"* to advertise the assigned block as soon as RIPE did. And the identifiers had to match.

The way we did it, we would wait for RIPE to confirm things on their end, and then we would modify things on our end, leading to

---

* Actually the Domain Name System, or DNS.

about a day's worth of delay in "lighting up" that IP space and propagating it to the network. I always wondered how that one competitor did it more quickly, and now, I thought I knew the answer.

I pointed my addressing and naming tool at their DNS server, and queried it in several different ways, and finally, I hit the jackpot – a number of hidden blocks of code that matched up with those obscured RIPE entries. Critically for my purposes, they included the identifier. In a way, they came up with a pretty clever way to ensure faster propagation of new connections, but it also gave me an opportunity.

I went back to RIPE and queried its databases with those identifiers, and voila! I had a list of the names of companies whose IP spaces our competitor was about to advertise – in other words, soon to be customers.

I was not really breaking into anything – all of these resources were public – and it was not a particularly clever hack, but make no mistake, this was indeed a business intelligence hack. In today's world, this kind of activity could land me behind bars. Back then, in another country … I did not even realize it was wrong until much later in life.

And it worked.

I called David and gave him the list.

***

A couple of days later, I get to the office and he almost jumps me at the doors.

"Barak! You have no idea, you're a hero!" he practically shouts.

"Huh?" I responded.

"The list you gave me! I was able to get a new customer out of it!"

"Huh?" I repeated, dumbfounded.

"The … list. The list of companies. That you. Gave me". David was growing impatient. "How did you do it?"

"What list? Oh, the one from …", it finally dawned on me what he was talking about. "I don't understand – why would you be able to sign them up? Weren't they already customers of <our competitor>?"

"No!" he exclaimed. "Not all of them, anyway! I called them all and managed to steal one of the deals! Man, this is great!" He was getting very excited. "Can you do it again?"

"I mean, sure I can … I can even automate it if you want", I replied.

You can be sure that this became my highest priority project for the day. By the next morning, the enterprise team got an emailed list of all newly preregistered allocations of IPs that our competitor had submitted to RIPE since the previous day, with company names and often, the relevant name of their business point of contact and even phone numbers included.

From what I came to learn, we ended up "stealing" several dozen enterprise customers that way over the next few months before someone on the other side must have figured out what was going on, and shut down the hole in their server.

***

There are so many other stories to tell in this arena, and I am certain that anyone with any decent amount of time in the field must have a pile of 'em. But before I move on to the perp – excuse me, human – side of things, I would like to share one last anecdote.

Some years ago, I happened to be an observer for a short time in a matter that ultimately involved for-profit hacking originating from eastern Europe. Why I mention it, though, is not because of the incident itself, but rather one of the documents that I became exposed to internally as part of this investigation.

It was written in German, and looked very much like an American style mergers and acquisitions (M&A) agreement between two parties. It included things like equity stakes post-merger, proportional profit allocations, and the like. So far, so good. Except for one thing: the two organizations involved were, in reality, the "business front" for professional hacker groups.

The amazing theory offered to me by one of the parties dealing with this matter, which admittedly would never occur to me but makes an odd, even compelling kind of sense, was that they did it this way so that the agreement could be enforceable by a German-speaking court.

And if this doesn't strike you as a remarkable illustration of the intersection between Security and Legal, nothing would.

3

PEOPLE BE PEOPLE, YO

Another day, another company.

Back in the day when I was still working mostly by myself, I was hired to help a company whose Chief Information Officer (CIO) knew me from a previous engagement I had with him elsewhere.

The first contract with them had me write up a report on whether, and if so how, they should tackle payment card industry (PCI) compliance, which as this fellow knew was right up my alley.

So I did that, and the report was received very favorably, and then the more exciting thing happened from my perspective, which was that I was able to proceed into an ongoing "virtual CISO" (vCISO, that is, virtual Chief Information Security Officer) agreement with them.

Why was it so exciting?

The reality is that back then there really was nobody else that was doing this sort of thing, at least not the way I was envisioning it, and I was trying to establish the validity of this approach, this notion of vCISO, in the marketplace. While I had already had a couple of such contracts in my repertoire by then, this was the first one that was put together the way I had come to perceive that it should be structured. That is to say, instead of simply being a full-time 1099* contractor,[†] or serving as a "times and material" consultant, this ongoing engagement was to be delivered as a part-time executive on a fixed retainer.

Put another way, that very contract was the first one where the foundations of my company's current business model were first cemented in an actual commercial engagement.

One particular challenge I had to face was that I was, to some degree, also stepping in to replace the company's former network and security manager.

---

* For non-American readers, this is the American tax code for independent contractors.
† AKA "we get the same thing for cheaper" in corporate parlance.

DOI: 10.1201/9781003133308-4

How so?

Because even today – and most certainly back then – security leadership is still primarily considered by most people as a technology position, ultimately a subset of the IT department (hence, "IT Security"). With all the big talk about security as a strategic element of corporate strategy, CISOs still by and large report into the CIO or Chief Technology Officer (CTO) organizations.

Yes, some shifts have occurred in the past few years, but ten or twenty years ago?

The kind of thinking that would place security leaders elsewhere was practically unheard of.

Being that this was the case, it also served to add to my excitement, because the role as I had crafted it for the purposes of the proposal for this engagement already captured the essence of it being strategic rather than tactical, even if nominally I was reporting to the CIO. After all, it was he who had brought me in.

All of this held true even if, admittedly, I was amusing mostly myself with these radical thoughts at that time. Proof, as they say, is in the pudding, and this particular pudding has taken many years since that first contract to make in decently large batches.

Anyway, back to our main story.

The recently departed (not as in "dead", just as in "left the company") security leader – let's call him Moe – was apparently both respected and somewhat feared within the organization. This is by no means an unusual reaction to security leaders in general. As an aside, I find it distasteful that so many folks in this field seem to delight in occupying this position of "feared authority figure", which only serves to perpetuate the cycle of failed leadership in Security.*

Our friend Moe thrived on it.

How do I know?

Because a few weeks into my assuming the role of vCISO for this company he was right there in my office, trying to scare me into buying things.

Turns out that he had joined a firm selling an early form of vulnerability scanning that was beyond the traditional network-based

---

* Average lifespan of CISO in their role: 21 months. Consider this footnote another teaser for my book *Why CISOs Fail*. Get it. You know you want to.

stuff, as well as functioning as a managed security services provider (MSSP), where they would engage in outsourced implementation and ongoing maintenance work in information security. He (naturally, I suppose) was convinced that our company, his previous employer, could benefit from their tools and services.

Prior to our meeting, legal counsel had told me in strict confidence that he was not sure if Moe could really be trusted, and that it was one of the reasons they were secretly happy for him to leave. But they were also afraid that he could somehow cause them harm. When I inquired about the kind of harm involved, he could not quite explain it. It was a sort of gut sense. I could respect that.

Being a security guy, I figured I would try and get to the bottom of it.

When we met, Moe seemed like a nice enough fellow, and he of course knew everything about the company and the technical details of its network and systems. He described with fair accuracy some of the ongoing operational issues that they were suffering from, and mapped those out to his new company's tools and services.

All fine so far. We were having a friendly chat, and as an aside, I asked him to tell me what he might recall from his recent history in the company to which it might be worth my time to pay particular attention.

He named off a few things we already knew about, although the level of detail was pretty impressive (and, in all honesty, a little frightening). Still, it was all turkey bacon.*

But then he said something that caught my attention in a rather big way.

He described a very explicit issue related to internal access controls, and how they created a particular exposure. He pointed out that having an MSSP like theirs to run the operational aspects of the network would help catch and remediate these kinds of deficiencies.

Which was all true.

Except that the fashion in which he described them was actually implemented a few weeks following his recent departure.

There was no legitimate way for him to know the current control environment unless he could somehow observe the changes we had

---

* As in, reasonably kosher. Yes, I just made that up. You're welcome.

made – or someone on the inside was feeding him this information. I was determined to get to the bottom of which of these two options it was in reality.

Following the meeting, I asked one of the folks in the company to help look around the systems for any unusual configurations.

It did not take very long to find out what was going on.

***

I asked Moe to come visit us again a couple of weeks later to have a chat with me. He was very confident when he walked in, pretty sure that we were going to get down to negotiations.

Hands got shook.

Beverages and snacks were offered.

Pleasantries were exchanged.

"Moe", I asked him, "I'm curious: that issue you mentioned, how did you find out about it?"

"Through our scanning platform", he replied, a bit smug.

"OK", I said, "but the issue is actually internal to the network. So unless you have some way into the network, your platform should not be able to see it".

"Well … uhhh …" he stumbled for words.

I waited patiently.

"I mean, it just did, so maybe it's not strictly internal? Maybe you have an external exposure?"

"Come on, man", I continued, "you know it is internal. In fact, you know a whole lot more, don't you?"

I pointed behind my back at the whiteboard, where I had written a word amongst a bunch of chicken scratch. He had not noticed it before.

He sure did now.

The word represented a user ID.

***

What Moe had done was, to me, inexcusable in the context of both security and ethics.

He created an account for himself when he left the company that would give him a backdoor and allow him to covertly maintain access into the company's internal systems.

Then he used it to probe the internal network and collect the information that he then used to make the case for selling his new company's scanning and MSSP services back to his old company. While none of it was overly malicious – his intent was to impress his new employer by selling services to his old employer – the mechanics and optics of how he went about it were … how shall I put it?

Let's see … there is a word for it.

Oh, right.

Now I remember.

Criminal.

Indeed, the actions that Moe took were undoubtedly in violation of several computer crime statutes.

I knew it and he knew it.

By the time we were having this conversation, I had already assembled the necessary audit trails to completely implicate him in this illegal intrusion. Furthermore, I had reached out to the FBI to describe the case, and had already confirmed with them that the US attorney would be willing to prosecute, as long as the company pressed charges.

After a couple of minutes of discomfort, Moe confirmed the user name, and what he did.

He was hosed.

I knew it and he knew it.

This sort of behavior is downright intolerable in my eyes, so after we concluded our meeting and I showed him out, I went to general counsel, whom I had already briefed, to get their approval to proceed with the authorities.

And it was then that I learned a lesson that I will never forget, and I have seen confirmed repeatedly over the many years since then. The lesson goes roughly like this:

The fear of negative publicity lets a lot of unethical people regularly get away with outrageously bad behavior.

Counsel asked me to verify that Moe no longer had any access to the environment, which I did (with the standard caveat of "to the best of my knowledge"). Then he told me that, after inquiring with senior leadership, they decided that, since no harm was done, they preferred to close this issue out quietly.

No harm, no foul.

Moe has since then built for himself a fairly successful career in the industry. To this day, he is doing deep technical security work within many brand name enterprises. I am willing to lay odds that he does not even remember the moment when I had him dead to rights, and he could have easily ended up behind bars with no career to speak of at all.

In fact, in what can only be described as the ultimate twist of irony, the company eventually decided to acquire services from Moe's new employer, because they felt that with Moe knowing so much about their systems, they would get better service (and, as counsel confided in me, they could be sure that he would not screw them; that fear factor was still very much present).

That they were essentially taken hostage into this decision seemed to be lost in the shuffle.

The Stockholm Syndrome got another notch in its ever-expanding belt.

***

Many people talk about security as being in the realm of "people" but, when asked to explain what they mean, often cannot come up with satisfactory answers. A common one involves the idea that "employees should follow policy better" which is an intellectually bankrupt position. If you decide to bet the security of your firm's most sensitive information assets on the capacity of all of its employees to consistently follow policies that they do not even care to read, then you deserve what's coming to you.

And no, it is not the employees' fault that they do not read the policy. Let's face it, most system administrators and engineers, not to mention a fair number of security professionals, do not do so either (even if they pretend otherwise).

For most people, policies are seriously boring.

Believing in the power of policy to drive better security is, charitably, simple laziness.

The reality is that human behaviors have an enormous impact on security, but in ways that we do not like to acknowledge. Employees are people, which means they* are complex, unpredictable, emotionally

---

* That is, *we*.

unstable, with motivations that cannot be easily determined and cannot be generally accounted for, no matter how much we like to think of them as "resources" that operate like other kinds of resources (AKA machines).

To be good in security you have to accept that the vast majority of your job will involve large helpings of uncertainty, at all times. Just like Moe in the story above, and the way all the people impacted by his actions reacted, and how it led to a frankly absurd end result. And people, not machines, are the way you will get hurt. That is how it is going to remain until a rogue artificial intelligence (AI) enslaves us all.

And one of the worst common offenses we all commit is in itself an incredibly human one; we tend to trust the people we like.

One day I was asked, in my capacity as vCISO in another place, to interview a candidate for the position of network manager. Considering the type of company involved, being a sort of ISP (Internet Service Provider), this was a critical position, and without question one of high trust. This person would have the mythical keys to the kingdom.

By the time I was going to speak with him, he had been interviewed by everyone else. My role was mostly restricted to a sanity check on the security side. The impression I got was that he was generally liked by the entire team, and was a shoo-in for the position.

Knowing my penchant for being unprepared – hey, it is true, no point in trying to hide it; I also generally do better speaking in panel formats than with, say, scripted presentations – I got the guy's resume about two minutes before the actual interview. As I quickly skimmed it, something was tugging at me, but I could not quite place a finger on what it was. I also did not have much time to dwell on it, as soon afterwards we got introduced, and had our chat.

The candidate came across as strong technically, very proud of his capabilities, and certainly with a strong depth of knowledge and expertise. Somewhat surprisingly, he also seemed like a pretty nice fellow, often a sticking point with folks in these professions and positions where their human interface may be lacking. A little reluctant to discuss with me specifically what made him seek a new position, maybe, but that can be normal if there is a history of personality clashes with a boss or something of that nature.

Nobody I know actually enjoys burning bridges, even if some people do it in anger.

But something still felt wrong.

We concluded our conversation, and I saw him out. Then I came back to the office I was occupying that day, and ran a Google search for him.

And there it was, right on the first page of search results.

No wonder he was uncomfortable; he had some time before been in the news after having left his previous employer while locking down their critical network infrastructure such that nobody could log in to it anymore. I was peripherally familiar with his name because I had read those stories when they were first published, and I guess the name stuck somewhere in my subconscious.

I showed these to the CIO, who was dumbfounded. They were getting ready to make him an offer, and if it were not for some dusty corner of my long term memory, he would have had a new opportunity to do the very same thing to them down the road. And because this was known, public information, there would be no way to say "we didn't know" if he did indulge himself in such behavior.

From my perspective, I wanted to figure out how he ended up even being invited to the interview in the first place. All I did was google his name, for heaven's sake.

We went to Human Resources.

Nobody wanted to own up to it, but it was clear that they never properly checked his background – they had apparently spoken to a reference he provided, but for all I could tell, did not really do anything else. Somebody had run a criminal background check but never bothered to read the resulting report, although in all fairness, that might not have helped, as the conviction related to that affair* seems to have occurred after the interview, at least from what I was able to piece together as I continued to follow the story.

Running a Google search of his name?

What a crazy idea.

Talk about dodging a bullet!

---

* You would be surprised – or maybe not? – at how often these kinds of processes diminish into checkbox exercises.

***

You would think that an experience like the one above is fairly rare, and maybe most folks in the field of security do not ever run into people with actual computer crimes in their background, but it is actually the opposite: it is not that uncommon for former blackhats* to then turn around and find gainful employment in the field, often after being caught, prosecuted, and convicted. Some of the most famous include the two Kevins, Mitnick and Poulsen (the latter of whom is now, amongst other brilliant endeavors, editor at Wired magazine).

Not that this guy was a hacker, mind you. He was a pissed off engineer who took action against his employer, a much more dangerous type of threat: the internal malicious user.

And he certainly was not my first.

A couple of years before then, as a vCISO for another company, I worked with Human Resources to implement a new background check process for employees in certain sensitive roles – including administrative technology staff. One of the key elements we introduced was that for people in these roles, we would perform the criminal portion recurringly, every two years, or whenever an employee moved into a sensitive role due to a promotion or internal job change. Incidentally, this is a critical control that so many organizations fail to implement. While I do not expect anyone to run background checks repeatedly on their entire workforce, I do think everyone understands that lives change, and bad things can happen to people ... including to employees in highly trusted positions.

In this case, when we ran the new batch on existing key employees, we got a ping.

It was for the IT systems administrator, the guy who controlled access to every critical back-office function, including IT, finance, HR, and legal – pretty much everything but the production environment. We will call him Gary.

It was a felony conviction.

---

* A "blackhat" refers to a hacker with criminal intent – the bad guys, the attackers. A "whitehat" is a hacker who works defensively by hacking the systems of targets and providing them the results so they can fix the vulnerabilities that a blackhat would otherwise exploit (also called a "penetration test"). Whitehats are also called ethical hackers. I won't get into the depressingly familiar issues surrounding the use of particular colors in these terms.

It was for computer crime.

It was recent – he had picked it up after the time he was initially hired.*

And nobody at all in the company knew anything about it.

It was time for an interview.

Now, let me make this clear: Gary was an extremely nice fellow, pleasant, well-liked by his peers, sociable, always eager to help, and overall just a picture of the perfect employee.

If you had to pick someone from the entire company to have this show up in a random background check, nobody would pick him.

He was highly trusted.

We talked. I had conducted enough interviews of a similar nature before, so expected a bit of back and forth before we could get to the bottom of things, but Gary surprised me. As soon as I explained the nature of the meeting, he came right out and told me the story. Out of respect to him I will not share most of the details, but in the end it came down to this: he was young, stupid, and did not entirely understand the consequences of his actions. The actual crime involved leaving himself a backdoor to one of his previous employer's systems, which he used as a file storage and exchange mechanism for himself (think of it as an early version of a personal cloud drive) over a period of time, and long after he had left that place of employment, until he was finally detected and caught. It was a clear case of unauthorized use, even if he did not otherwise cause any harm to the organization (except for the purloined storage space).

His previous employer decided to press charges, the case was referred to the FBI, and that was how he ultimately ended up with a felony.

By the time the interview ended, I actually felt torn. It was clear that Gary had no malicious intent against his former employer, but at the same time, that he made a conscious, informed decision to do something that he knew was wrong. He did not properly understand the qualitative nature of "wrong", and his underestimation ultimately

---

* That does not mean that the related crime happened after he was hired, of course, only that the criminal proceedings involving the crime had reached some legal conclusion by that time. It does, however, indicate that he knew about it when he got hired, and did not disclose it – just like that other guy in the previous example.

led to a criminal conviction. Unlike the fellow from the previous story, I did not think he was the kind of person who would set out to cause actual harm, and with some mentoring, he could end up doing quite well down the road.

Still, with a computer crime on his record, and with sentencing still to follow, the risk to his present employer was obviously too great. I ended up with the unpleasant task of having to inform him that he was being let go, even as I felt deeply sorry for him.

That feeling was certainly not what I expected when I first walked into the interview!

Later on, I was asked to provide a written opinion as part of his sentencing hearing, and found myself again having to make a difficult judgment call. I ended up trusting my impression from the interview and recommending an easier sentence and a focus on rehabilitation. I of course have no idea if my input made any difference, but Gary did ultimately receive a sentence on the lighter side of the guidelines. Afterwards, he managed to find his way back into the industry, even as he stayed brutally honest about his conviction; the very same odd foundation of integrity that initially took me by surprise about him during that interview.

***

How to handle findings from background checks is a heavily fraught topic, especially considering the elements of social inequity that manifest themselves therein, but I still find it odd that so many organizations treat them with suspicion. I tend to fall on the side of wanting to know, even if I have to deal with the consequences, which when I think about it, is probably a reflection of my chosen career.

But sometimes you do not even need those checks.

In another case, an employee (let's go with Roman) at one of our customers approached me. We had struck a friendship while I was there, and had developed a high level of mutual trust. Around that time, I had made an internal recommendation to move him away from his system administration position into a security-focused role. The next day, we went for a post-prandial walk outside, and it was clear that something was troubling him. I already knew that the best way to deal with it was simply let him get to it in time, so we chatted about life in general for a bit.

Then, a few minutes into our walk, he changed the subject.

"Barak", he started, "I have to tell you something, but I'm really afraid of saying it".

"Afraid?" I asked. It sounded pretty ominous.

"Yes", he said. Then he added, "but I trust you, and I know I would not be able to live with myself if I didn't tell you about it".

He went on to tell me about his own fairly recent drug conviction. How it happened is not really relevant to this story, but it did eventually result in a criminal record, a fine, and some community service. People do stupid things, and sometimes those stupid things catch up with them, and this was a classic example. A few years later, his record would be cleansed following a change in the law in California, but we had no way of knowing that this would ultimately happen when he brought it up to my attention.

His concern was that moving into a security role, reporting to me (since I was not an employee, he had a different personnel manager at the company, but I would direct his work), would create a difficult and potentially contentious situation. He had never informed the company of any of this happening, and this was one of the many organizations which sucked at background checks, so there was zero chance of them ever picking it up themselves. I would likely never discover it either. But his inner sense of right and wrong led him to tell me about it anyway, because he felt (admirably) that security is a field that required higher standards. Then he added that he did not want to cause me any trouble. He knew that I had made the recommendation for the internal role transition, and if this came out, that I might be embarrassed.

He did not want that to happen.

I was unduly impressed, and more than a little grateful. Talk about moral fiber!

Now that I knew about it, I of course had to let the company know, but relying on every ounce of trust that I myself had established with the company's leadership, and because of the nature of the offense, he was not let go and still moved into the new role, where he remained and did an excellent job for many years afterwards.

All of that, though, is not why I bring up Roman's story.

A couple of years later, in my role as mentor to him, Roman told me that he finally felt ready to tackle the industry's most respected certification – the Certified Information Systems Security Professional (CISSP), issued by "ISC Squared" (ISC²)*. I had held this certification for a long time, so I knew what his problem was, and he immediately confirmed it: it did not require just trade skills. ISC² also has a strong code of professional ethics, which they enforce pretty strictly, and he was afraid that his criminal record would bar him from being accepted even if he passed their already fairly difficult exam.

Nervously, he asked me for advice. He was savvy enough to know that if he never disclosed this to them, the likelihood of their ever finding out was also extremely small. In that, he was right; I could not imagine a scenario where he would be "discovered" unless he did something bad in security that would lead to an investigation of his past. In reality, even that conclusion was overly pessimistic, seeing as his record was scrubbed clean not too long later due to the aforementioned change in California law.

So he was right in theory, but he did not feel good about it.

He did not want to lie.

But he also really wanted that certification.

My advice to him, which to a degree was inspired by Gary from the previous story, was this: he could choose to take one of two paths. One of them – where he would not disclose this matter – would be easier, and practically guaranteed to succeed. But knowing him, it would eat at him internally forever. He would feel like a fraud, and no matter how well he might end up doing in his career in the security field, that feeling would never leave him.

The second path had risk – primarily that he might fail to attain the certification he so desired, even if he otherwise passed the test, and provably had all the necessary skills and background. But doing it that way would guarantee him peace of mind, secure in the knowledge that when he did get certified even with full disclosure, it would be well earned and could not be challenged.

I also volunteered to assist. You see, the way ISC² handles certifications, a new member receiving their highest honor would have to be sponsored by an existing member in good standing. I had

---

* If you wonder what that "squared" business means, the full name of the organization is the International Information System Security Certification Consortium – stare at it for a moment, I promise that it will come to you.

sponsored a few folks over the years, so I was quite familiar with the process. I told Roman that if he chose the first path, I could not endorse him, but if he chose the second, I would not only endorse him, but write a letter on his behalf explaining my reasoning, my insight into his character, and why I thought he should be certified even with that blemish on his record. My opinion was that he would ultimately prevail.

Then I left him with the choice.

Eventually, he chose to trust me and my faith in the organization, and went with full disclosure. He passed his exam, and sent in all the materials, noting his drug conviction and attaching my supporting letter. Then it was time to wait.

Typically, this process takes a few weeks, maybe a month or so. But a month passed, then two, then three, and Roman was growing increasingly worried sick with shame. The pain of it was all too real. He knew, just knew, that he would be rejected. It did not matter how many times I tried to remind him that this was an unusual situation, and that the organization would likely take quite a while to work through it; he anticipated the worst, and every day, week, and month made it even worst-ier.

You can probably guess what eventually happened; ISC^2 ultimately and sensibly chose to certify him and he has been a proud member in good standing ever since. His gratitude after he learned of their decision was almost overwhelming. But the most pleasing aspect for me, personally, was his acknowledgment of the value of maintaining his integrity throughout the process, and his own sense of self-worth. He told me as much: "Barak, now I know that I really turned the corner, that no matter how stupid I was before, this is real and it means so much to me".

Who knew that an industry certification, no matter how significant, could hold so much emotional value?

*****

I am sharing all these stories with you because I think they highlight an important point that seems to have gone missing in corporate America, namely that people are not just "resources" to be "managed", and you cannot reduce humans to machine equivalent, no matter how much more comfortable it might be to imagine doing so. Critically, there will always be tension between the need to trust your employees to behave properly, and the absolute, guaranteed, gold plated certainty that some of them will not.

To me, it is one of the most, shall we say, endearing aspects of our general rose colored glasses view of the world that we tend to think of the Human Resources department's role as that of "supporting the workforce". You already know I am not one to mince words, so let me make my opinion clear: this is a load of horseshit, baloney, and utter nonsense. HR has one, and only one, primary job in a typical American corporation: to *protect the company from its employees* and the various and sundry liabilities they may create.

Period.

The rest is window dressing.

The way this translates into security is that any approach that depends on "employees behaving well" is doomed to fail at some point, 100% of the time. You want to know why your precious user awareness posters do not work and are never going to work? Why tailgating is so effective? Why people (including big-name CEOs) still leave laptops with sensitive company information on the table at Starbucks when they go the bathroom? Why the old style, ancient technology hacking vector of slipping someone an envelope full of cash is still so gosh darn effective?

Simple.

Because humans.

You can try to solve it with process, something an organization like the National Security Agency (NSA) does fairly well, but even there, you still get the occasional Edward Snowden. Apple's research and development (R&D) department is a prime private industry example, which very few can afford to emulate, and yet leaks still happen.

You get my point.

I still remember the earnest instructions I received very early in my career from an extremely senior technology person at the company I worked for. Larry* was assigned to mentor me through my transition from front line customer support to helping design and run the network infrastructure, and I acquired many valuable skills and knowledge from him. Yet even back then I was developing a deep interest

---

* Yes, yes, not his real name. Again.

in the behavioral aspect of security, and this one conversation we had really stuck in my mind as a remarkable example that I knew I would end up sharing in some distant future.

Welcome to the future!

It was a few months into our collaboration and Larry clearly felt that he could trust me. So one afternoon when we were sitting in the otherwise empty company cafeteria, and going over some of the day's network events, he started talking in the instructional tone that I had come to appreciate – the one he used to give me a larger perspective about the job, role, and career in which I had been taking my first steps.

He was trying to give me insights into how to ensure that you would always be considered valuable, so that you would not be at risk of losing your job.

But what he actually said was, in retrospect, pretty stunning.

He advised that, as the person in charge of the infrastructure, he would occasionally generate little disruptions that people would notice, and then he would fix them and be the hero. "You see", Larry said, "if everything keeps running smoothly, then nobody will appreciate you; this is how you remind them that you exist and you are important and they can't live without you".

I was very young back then and had a lot of admiration for him, so I spent some time considering this proposition, ultimately rejecting it. But can I say that it did not make a certain kind of sense?

Of course it did.

Because we ... are ... human.

And if you think there aren't quite a few Larrys out there, in highly trusted roles, then you are viewing the world through the same comfortable rose-colored glasses.

***

I am going to end this chapter with one last misbehaving human, whose actions were breathtaking in their brazenness.

Their chutzpah.

We will call him Dwight.

Dwight was an attempt by this particular company to replace me as their vCISO with a full-time employee in the CISO role. This is not unusual, and is often the natural progression if a company grows large enough, but in their case, they were still fairly small. However, this was still pretty early in my development of the vCISO role in general, so I was perhaps not that good at it yet, and they felt like they were growing very rapidly and wanted to insource the management function.

They kept me on as an advisor to support Dwight, and continue to oversee the PCI compliance program, which I knew better than anyone else, while getting Dwight up to speed so he could ultimately own that program as well.

Dwight seemed like a likable enough guy, although he had some personality quirks. In the field of technology, and especially Security, this is not unusual; people and social skills are simply not expected of us nerds. In Dwight's case, he had an odd tendency to keep his face frozen in all manners of conversation – he could in fact smile and even laugh, so to the best of my knowledge it was not a physical disability, but usually all you got was a singular expression that never changed, no matter the topic. He was a martial arts expert and used to practice in the parking lot most days, which came off as a bit weird as well. But maybe the biggest telling point was that he never volunteered information about himself, even when prodded, usually a fairly important component of trust and relationship building.

We went through one audit together, then spent the next few months with me as a mentor to Dwight, until he let me know that he felt comfortable that he could navigate the next audit by himself. It was time for me to step back and let him run with it, which was welcome news as I had already allocated my time to other customers.

I checked in with him a few times but his responses were confident and reassuring, and I had no reason to think that anything was going wrong. He said everything was done and all the documentation submitted, and then the holidays were upon us.

The first sign that something was wrong was when Steve,* the QSA† on the engagement, reached out to me after the new year. I had known Steve for a number of years and I was the one who brought him and his company in to this customer to perform the PCI audits.

---

* Real name, for once.
† Qualified Security Assessor, which is the official term for "PCI auditor" in the world of PCI.

"Barak", he asks me, "do you know when we are going to get the rest of the evidence?"

"What evidence?" I ask him back, surprised.

"For the PCI audit", he says. "So we can finish it", he adds, in that tone you use sometimes with particularly difficult people.

My mouth fell open.

I did not know what to say. Dwight had assured me that the audit was done at least two months beforehand, and I was not involved in the process except to answer his questions.

I told Steve as much.

"Well," he said, "we still need ..." and went on to list a set of evidence that was never provided to them. And as he worked down the list, my heart sank. These were the most difficult ones, the security operations bits that required diligence in producing (since they reflected actual, recurring tasks that needed tracking) as well as collecting and organizing for submission. If you had ever undergone a PCI (or, for example, SOC2 type 2) audit, you will know exactly what those are.

If you have not, then be grateful.

So I reached out to the executive to whom I was still reporting internally (hmm ... let's make it a Ken for this one), in my much-diminished role as advisor. He said he had no idea, but would reach out to Dwight and let me know as soon as the first full week in January started and he was back in from vacation.

I relayed this to Steve and we waited.

One of the problems in "PCI world" is that compliance reporting is actually enforced with a fair amount of strictness. You can usually get a 90-day extension for your annual reporting,* but going beyond that can be uncomfortable, and can lead to financial penalties levied by the credit card associations. These guys were already almost three months behind. They basically had until the end of the month to get it done.

The weekend came and went, and it was around the middle of the following week when I finally heard back from Ken.

"Barak", he tells me in a grave tone, "we have a problem".

"What's going on?"

---

* And you better believe that some companies had been trying to use this to create a recurring 15-month cycle for themselves, because, again, humans.

"We can't get a hold of Dwight. And nobody has any clue where he is. Can you come by?"

***

It took about two weeks to get through the next bit, which was pretty exciting or devastating, depending on your point of view.

The first thing I did was ask another person to locate the server where most of that recurring data was collected automatically. See, before I stopped running the program, we had it set up such that various systems would deposit certain key evidence into that server. This way, when audit time came, they would be easy to obtain and provide to the auditor. So regardless of where Dwight might be, it should have been easy to grab this stuff.

That was when we discovered the next problem.

Dwight had locked down the server.

And I do not mean he changed the password to his account, or the account that I previously had, or the one that was set up for emergencies. No. He actually removed every single account except his own. There was no way to access the server without him.

While we could try and obtain information off it using forensic methods, the company was nervous – that well-known fear of breaking something that nobody fully understands freezing them from taking immediate action.

So we launched a project to reconstruct what we could from source systems, and I started working with Steve on how to explain what was missing in a manner that would be acceptable for PCI auditing purposes.

In the meantime, I also joined the search for the missing Dwight. Many of us were worried that maybe something bad had happened to him during the holidays, and the concern levels were high. Remember that Dwight was extremely private; no one knew much about his personal life, and it turned out that he did not leave a legitimate emergency contact.

***

Being well connected can have its drawbacks. For example, it can be quite impossible to actually return all the messages one regularly receives from one's numerous connections, let alone strangers. But it confers some advantages when dealing with this kind of situation. That I am a peculiar bird with my affinity towards the go-to market side of the business, even though I ply my trade in a well-established corner of nerdworld, helps as well. Because if you want a particularly effective way to find something about someone in the industry, well ...

Ask some sales people.

They know.

So I dropped some feelers, and waited.

It did not actually take that long.

The following week, a friend of mine, an enterprise sales person at a security vendor, called me and asked if Dwight, whom I had introduced to him to give him a chance to try and make a sale, had left his job.

"Why?" I asked.

"Well", he said, "because I just had lunch with him at" – and here he gave the name of a company I had never heard of before. "He was running the security department and was looking into buying our stuff".

So I looked up this new organization he mentioned. You might think that it would be easy enough, but information was not readily available. Ultimately, with a bit of digging, I managed to figure out that it was a new technology startup still in stealth mode. And that our friend Dwight was indeed working there, as the Director of Security.

Basically, Dwight was collecting two paychecks simultaneously.

He never bothered to notify the people at his "other" present employer, the one I was helping, of his departure. And for whatever sick reason he may have had, he really screwed them with locking out that server.

I notified Ken and waited for the fireworks to erupt.

And now, based on everything I have shared with you up to this point, let me ask you this – what do you think happened? Did Dwight lose his new job? Did he get sued? Did he get in any kind of trouble at all?

If your answer was a resounding "NO" then go right ahead and reward yourself with an ice cream cone.

Sure, the folks at my client organization were happy and grateful with my discovery of the location of "Wayward Dwight". But when

I tried to suggest gently that they could easily pursue some action against this extremely unethical person, I ran into the very same wall of fear that I had encountered before – and since. Dwight knew too much. Dwight could really hurt them if he became angry. They did not want to be in the news.

Instead, they disabled his accounts, terminated his employment, and brought me back in to run security as a vCISO. They also reached out to him via the new cellphone number that I had provided (bless that sales rep's heart) and asked him nicely to return his laptop, which in a surprise twist, he actually did a couple of weeks later – but only after he forced them to agree not to try and recoup the wages they had paid him while he was working elsewhere, and allow him to cash out his vacation and sick time as well.

As for the server? By the time Dwight "graciously agreed" to unlock it for us, we no longer needed it. The compliance project was back on track, and the company was overjoyed that they avoided fines and penalties from the credit card associations. Steve and I simply told those folks the truth – that an administrator went rogue and nuked their access to logs and other material, so they had to start over. In return we got a further 90-day extension to collect and present at least a quarter's worth of necessary evidence, and this was sufficient to get by that audit. But let me tell you, the exchanges with the card association folks made for one amusing – or terrifying, depending on your perspective – paper trail.

***

As you can see by now with these stories of real people doing real people things, Gary's outcome was notably different, and mostly because his former employer was hard-nosed about it, and did not care whether it would make the news. That made them the exception rather than the rule. If you were to ask me, Gary's offense was the most trivial of all of the ones I had shared with you here (and many others I could add), and yet he was the only one to have been punished.

He was simply unlucky.*

And the point is, as many an officer of the law will tell you, that this is pretty much par for the course. We all know that most everyone

---

* Security is a discipline where luck plays a remarkably prominent role.

steals office supplies, but at least with physical objects, there is a more immediate sense of guilt associated with the action, the fear of being caught.

You can bet your sweet ass that when the landscape is virtual, unethical behaviors become more pronounced.

Not less.

Which leads us into our next couple of chapters, and a question that intrigues me: what happens when the folks who make decisions are so invested in being right, that it leads to bad outcomes? And what happens when their area of expertise is not only foreign, but even scary to most of their peers?

When it comes to software security, the results can be downright fascinating.

4

Designer Goods

As fond as I am of saying that Security is not a technology discipline, the truth is that technology plays a big role in security as a discipline. Infosec is very much grounded in technology, and people often understand Security as something that has to do with Information Technology (IT*), even if they otherwise understand very little about security of data in general. That's OK; it is part of the evolution of any discipline from being something that is niche-y into an actual, legitimate part of successfully operating a business.

We can think back to the world of IT itself and the emergence of the role of the Chief Information Officer (CIO†) back in the Eighties and Nineties. Security today, and the similarly and seemingly explosive emergence of the Chief Information Security Officer (CISO‡), mimic to a large degree what we saw three and four decades ago with respect to technology in general, and especially with the Internet as a new and exciting growth catalyst. Then we had the promise of the paperless office, a big one from the Eighties that is really only being fulfilled today following the arrival on the scene of large scale, back-office cloud services. Amusingly, these services themselves offer a striking parallel to the world of mainframes and dumb terminals back in the good ol' days stretching all the way back to the Sixties.

Be that as it may, and to pull us back into the present, we often see security problems emerge in the context of technology. And one area in which security and technology intersect extremely strongly is encryption.

Encryption is a big deal.

We rely on encryption to keep our information safe when we connect to websites, for example. In the legal realm, if you have ever had

---

* Yes, I know you know.
† Again, I know you know.
‡ Last time, I promise.

DOI: 10.1201/9781003133308-5   **83**

to look at a contractual clause that obligates a vendor to implement at least this version or that of Secure Socket Layer (SSL*) or Transport Layer Security (TLS†) at a minimum in order to secure traffic, you were observing a common example of security routinely intersecting with both legal and of course, the IT folks who are running the website in the background.

Other examples include hashing passwords or keeping them encrypted, the latter of which, incidentally, is a bad idea. Encrypting passwords means that they can be reversed into their unencrypted form, and there is generally no reason to do that in authentication systems. Instead, a system that maintains and therefore wishes to keep passwords stored safely should use a "one way" (hashing) algorithm to arrive at a scrambled (hashed) value of the password. Every time that a user attempts to use that password, the system simply uses the same algorithm and just matches the resulting scrambled value with the one it had stored previously.

Needless to say, the algorithm does not in fact allow for unscrambling the underlying stored password, on account of its particular mathematical properties. That is where the "one way" part comes into play; when you use hashing, the math driving this process guarantees that an original value – like a password – will always "translate" to the same gobbledygook (hash) if you run it through the hashing exercise, but unlike in encryption, you cannot take the gobbledygook and reverse it back into the original password.‡ This is safer for the users because their passwords are not actually stored in the system; therefore, if it gets compromised and the file full of hashes is stolen, the attacker still will not have access to the users' original passwords.

This serves, therefore, as another common example of the intersection of security and technology, in the realm of encryption.

---

* A protocol for encrypting data transmissions that pretty much served as a foundation for the Internet for a good couple of decades. Chris Allen, one of the inventors of SSL, is part of my boardgaming group. Why would you care? I have no idea, except that he's a cool guy, it ties to a different footnote from earlier in the book, and extranerdy name dropping is fun!

† A more modern protocol replacing SSL, because SSL is now considered "broken" in security parlance, that is, it is susceptible to attack and thus no longer capable of being secure.

‡ With caveats. There are always caveats ... but let's roll with it for now.

Encryption plays another role, and a very important one, in protecting copyrightable content, via Digital Rights Management (DRM*). DRM schemes are basically intended to support the need of content creators to protect their content. DRM is a critical piece of a fair number of industries, especially when we have moved wholesale into electronic distribution of content such as e-books, streaming music and television shows, and other forms of easily consumed content. The need to protect such content from being copied easily for pirated use is a big driver behind DRM for the companies whose business models revolve around capturing content-related revenue.

Because DRM is such a big deal, there is a whole field of expertise surrounding the use of proper encryption methodologies, such as digital signing and various forms of hashing within the DRM world. And this finally† brings us to our first story in this chapter.

The company in question was a very large one, a Fortune-500 multinational, and they had plenty of content they needed to protect. They were both producing and acquiring such content from a large number of content creators and essentially redistributing it in different forms. Some of these distribution methods were digital and implemented via both commonly available devices manufactured by others, as well as devices that they manufactured and sold themselves. DRM, in this context, was clearly a very big deal. And because DRM was a big deal, they wanted to make sure that they were doing it the right way.

In other words, while we were consulting with them on other matters, it was inevitable that the DRM issue would eventually cross our path.

And so, one day we were invited to this engineering meeting. And in the meeting they were discussing their new implementation of DRM within the context of their content acquisition, management and distribution ecosystem. The folks in the meeting were high-level senior engineers and business leaders, and they were describing the DRM scheme, which is when, as they say, our ears done got perked.

The reason was that what they were proposing to do appeared to replicate an unfortunate and rather common mistake in the world of

---

* I lied earlier when I said it was the last one. But … aren't you in acronym heaven?
† "Took you long enough, Barak. This ain't the Discovery channel, ya know" … yeah, I can see your thought bubble.

encryption. It is an easy mistake to make, because it is one of those situations where you seem to be following the rules, but happen to be ignorant of some of the side effects; a scenario where one knows "just enough to be dangerous", if you will.

In this particular case, in order to develop a proper signature for a particular piece of content stored on a device belonging to a particular end-user, which they could consider a sort of watermark, the team designed a hash function that would produce a unique value. That hash value was constructed, as is typical, by combining various strings of clear text, a fairly common approach, and the algorithm itself was taken from proven, well tested public libraries.

So far, so good.

Upon inquiry, we were told that the hash value was constructed using three distinct elements: the first name and last name of the consumer as well as the credit card number used for the purchase. The credit card number was, of course, discarded after the hashing process was done, so there would be no way to retrieve it. Doing it this way apparently gave them some distinct benefits in terms of easily being able to uniquely associate each license with its consumer owner.

So far, so good.

Except that, of course, that it was not actually that great. Because while designing all this, they ended up introducing an unexpected side effect, which in turn resulted in the unintended consequence of nullifying any crypto* benefit from the scheme.

Can you guess what it was?

If you do not have sufficient background in this area, I doubt you would be able to. If you do, however, then you are already rolling your eyes.

What they did was store the first and last name of the consumer who owned the device alongside the computed hash value in the same record within the app's database.

Now, that does not sound too bad, does it?

Oh, but I assure you, it is bad. Very, very bad.

---

* "Crypto" is short for "cryptographic" and essentially means "encryption", but sounds way cooler.

The problem with it, as any crypto expert will tell you,* is that the moment when you start storing portions of the plaintext† next to the computed hash value is the moment you start weakening the strength of the hashing function. And in this case, the problem quickly became acute, because the hashing function itself was, by necessity, stored alongside the hash value within the device. This would give an attacker not only a partial plaintext to work with, but also the structure and size of the plaintext, and the block size used by the function.

In other words, some of those essential, and normally hidden, mathematical properties.

We politely pointed out that there may be a slight problem with this methodology. That storing the hash value together with portions of the plaintext weakens the hashing function considerably. That it could even make it trivial to recover the plaintext. That doing it this way is, not to put too fine a point on it, generally a big no-no. Unsurprisingly, the folks who had already built the scheme into the product did not actually know any of that, but at the same time, they kind of did not want to believe us.

What they actually said was, "hey, you know what, we don't exactly understand. Hashing is one-way, isn't it?"

And here we come to face one of the big problems with encryption, in that it is really difficult to implement encryption properly, for the simple reason that it is generally pretty hard to understand. Even when using tested, publicly available algorithms, people fail to do this correctly all the time (check out the next story). This team was indeed using strong algorithms and they felt that the mechanism was great without understanding the underlying mathematics and resulting implications of what can happen to that strong algorithm if you store portions of the plaintext next to it.

---

* ... and the one we got to write the report for them to tell them about it is in fact a bonafide world class authority on crypto.

† The cool kid's way of saying "the original text that was being encrypted or hashed in the first place".

After all, one way is one way, right?* (Note that this is how engineers do think: something either is or is not. This is the cause of many, many painful misunderstandings in the world of technology.)

And so we proposed that we would prove it to them.

One benefit of working with these very large companies is that unexpected budgeting can occasionally be secured for atypical purposes, if they are important to the business. This was, and so we retained a hacker, if you will. Actually he was – and still is – a world-renowned authority on cryptography, but in this context, he effectively served as a hacker. We asked him to do an analysis for us and write a report to the company, either confirming that their approach was valid or, as we suspected, showing how quickly it was possible to break their hashing scheme and obtain the full clear text (with that credit card number) from the hash value.

Could he, for all intents and purposes, reverse the hashing function?

The fascinating thing in all this was not that we were right; my own rudimentary understanding of crypto was enough to know that we were, and it was why we insisted that the scheme might be broken in the first place. It was that we got the report back extremely quickly. It simply did not take very long for the esteemed gentlemen to perform this task (I spoke with him later, since he is also a friend of mine, and he laughingly admitted that it was so weak it took all of a couple of hours in one afternoon† to figure it out and then write a 60-line script that automated the hack).

Here is what the report said: the computational element of all this – the meat, the "how long did it take me to break this stuff?" part – the report, which was very detailed, basically showed that pretty much

---

* The reason that hashing is "one way" is a topic of many a book, so I won't get into that here. Suffice it to say that it relies on the idea that many different plaintexts will produce the same hash value ("many-to-one") and so even given that value, it's impossible to revert to the specific original plaintext that generated it. Having portions of the plaintext narrows down dramatically the possible search space for finding that original plaintext for that specific function.

† Incidentally, that's why people who actually know what they are doing are worth their hourly weight in gold; you're not just paying for their time. You're paying for the decades of expertise that makes the time they spend on the problem so, so much more efficient. I mention this because it took me a long time to accept that my own time is worth as much as it is, which is a lot, and somebody whom I really cherish in my life really had to explain this to me (read: hammer it into my head) at some point.

anybody with a mainstream, decent laptop could run that 60-line script against that DRM scheme and crack or reverse the hashing of any particular value within seconds or at worst, minutes. And of course, all those credit card numbers would then be extracted because once you reversed the hash value, you would get the full original text, which, as you recall, was constructed from the consumer's first name, last name, and credit card number.

Fixing this would require a rethinking of their entire approach to DRM. It would not be technically difficult to implement, but it would take a fair bit of engineering effort, and overhauling a few other systems (including a devil of a large complex database) and code repositories that were already built based on the existing assumptions of how things were going to work in the product.

So how do you think they took it?

Exactly as you might expect.

The engineers were still suspicious; if the function was not truly one way then how could they trust that it would hold up even if the whole thing was rebuilt from scratch? The idea that a mathematical property could be constrained based on the conditions in which it was being operated was somewhat anathema to this group of software developers, whose world is filled with absolute directives. Plus they felt that it made them look bad.

Why should they trust us?

What do we – we were consultants, after all – know?

The business leaders – the ones who were ultimately in charge of rolling this out to support a worldwide launch of their new hardware device – were horrified, but not by the report; rather, they were predictably (and rightfully) concerned by the possible delay any sort of retrofit would introduce to the launch. And let me tell you,* there is nothing better in the whole wide world than being the reason behind this sort of unexpected delay.

Especially if you are a consultant.

And, as you might imagine, our executive sponsor was getting all sorts of feedback, and, uhh, not all of it was, shall we say, pleasant.

Having delivered our report, we did what any experienced security person learns to do in moments like this, which was to assume an

---

* Sarcasm mode – ON.

innocent face,* and go to lunch. We did not actually expect that this would ever get fixed, and most certainly not before the new product launch. Infosec being the field that it is, that is, full of dire predictions that usually do not come true but have to be explicitly stated anyway, it was ultimately unlikely that anyone would pay a price for a "go ahead" decision. By the time the bad scenario would play out, if it ever did,† the folks involved in making the original decision would be long gone, either through promotions or job transitions to other companies. In that sense, the whole thing was a little bit like actual politics.

And so, as you probably figured out by now, they decided to "fix this with a patch later". I cannot tell you whether "later" ever arrived; in the two years we were still there following the issuance of the report, it had not. I can, however, tell you that the DRM scheme itself was in fact broken by a malicious player at some point. It is just that by that time, it did not matter very much, as the company itself had gotten into significant trouble, and the line of devices that they had been manufacturing which utilized this embedded scheme had by then become obsolete.

The world of technology, as we know, can move awfully fast.

***

The reason I told you this story is not because it ended up in disaster – it mostly did not, for all I can tell, because they had bigger issues – but rather, to point out that this sort of decision making around information security is fairly common. It happens every day, pretty much everywhere, which is after all the theme for this book. Taken individually, each such decision may seem perfectly reasonable, but put together, across the entire landscape of networks and infrastructures … well, there is a reason why hacking is so profitable.

It is, in fact, a direct outcome from one of the most fundamental principles of proper security management, as it is understood today: that security should be managed according to risk. Go ahead, look it

---

* Also known as "don't shoot the messenger".

† This would require a hacker to (a) figure out that there was a problem in the first place; and (b) decide it's worth their effort to capitalize on it. While the total amount of credit card accounts potentially compromised this way was large – in the eight or even nine figures – the underlying issue was fairly esoteric, and there are easier targets out there to go after.

up. Risk management is the foundation of the most respected standards, the best books, the talks by top speakers in the field. We can't fix it all, the theory goes, and therefore we should focus on things according to the risk they present.

This is all well and fine, and makes perfect sense, but for those of us who understand security a little differently, as an adjunct people discipline, it leads to predestination: the decision of what constitutes an acceptable risk, or how it should be prioritized, is of course made by people. And people can never be impartial arbiters. People will often downplay risk because other things matter more, or the negative outcome is highly unlikely, and we generally all suck at this game.* In one obvious example, we think nothing of driving our cars, a highly risky activity in comparison to taking a commercial flight, an activity of which quite a few of us are petrified.

The reality, of course, is that all of these judgment calls, of which many are made daily across all organizations, are just that: judgment calls, no matter how many pretty charts and complicated formulas we put around them. And the vast majority of them play out the way we anticipated them to play out, further reinforcing and inflating our sense of having made the right calls. But the law of large numbers dictates that some of these bad scenarios will in fact play out, and when they do, well …

Fairly recently, Solarwinds, FireEye, and Equifax come to mind, but I am sure that even if you have never been in the security field yourself, you can think of many others.

***

All of this leads me to another story, in a similar vein to the last one, but having its own set of interesting characteristics.† It involves another company I had worked with. What they were doing was developing a product that allowed people to communicate privately in a group setting, similar to various chat tools that everybody might be familiar with. It was, after a fashion, an early and less sophisticated version of Slack and other group collaboration software tools. In what was a pretty innovative approach for its time, it also supported

---

* Recall my Dudley story from Chapter 1 as a very personal example.
† Don't they all?

audio and video streaming. And in their case, they also provided some transactional capabilities and had some other nifty and fairly early innovations.

The company was growing pretty fast for a while and the tool became pretty popular in some parts of the world, and had a large and fast-growing user base that ultimately grew to hundreds of millions. One of the things they wanted to do was to make sure that all of these communications were very secure.

Now, in today's world, that sounds pretty obvious. We expect even common free tools like Yahoo Chat* or Skype to encrypt our communications and keep them safe, but back then, this was not necessarily the case. Many of these tools, even the two that I just mentioned, may not have had that sort of encryption capability built into them at the time, certainly not if you weren't paying a fee for them.

But these guys were a little more forward-thinking and they wanted to do the right thing, and make sure that all the communications were properly encrypted and secured. This is, of course, a good thing, although the impetus for it was due to a quirk of the nature of their growth, which was concentrated in regions of the world where users had reason to be more wary of government oversight of their private communications.[†]

Anyways, they ended up implementing a standardized encryption methodology for every message flying through the platform in any type of conversation or transaction, which was when they ran into a performance issue.

The cost of encryption was too high.

When I say "cost" in this context, I am not referring to dollars, but rather the performance penalty that resulted from adding encryption. This is a well-known phenomenon; back when I was still in Israel working for Netvision, that Internet Service Provider, and implementing transmission encryption selectively for certain types of sensitive communications, we used to call this the "encryption VAT",[‡]

---

* Here I go, dating myself again.

† And no, I'm not talking about the NSA and Ed Snowden. Ha ha, very funny.

‡ Value Added Tax, something that does not exist in the US but is fairly popular in other parts of the world; it's basically a tax on consumption paid at the register.

because the performance hit more or less equaled the actual Israeli VAT at the time, which was 17%.

Simply put, for these guys, adding encryption created too big of a delay in communications.

In beta, as we found out later, this issue made it so that the tool was essentially unusable because folks who were testing it were mentally comparing it to the experience they had with the unencrypted version (or of other popular tools, those without encryption); if conversations exhibited even a slight but still noticeable delay, their user satisfaction would plummet and they would end up migrating elsewhere. It also negatively impacted their total throughput for the platform.

This was clearly a serious business blocker.

Still, they wanted encryption and perceived it as essential to their success.

What to do?

What to ... do?

What they ended up doing is something that, as I mentioned in the previous story, is unfortunately both more common than we like to imagine, and also a huge crypto no-no.

While still using publicly available secure encryption libraries, they essentially developed their own crypto stack.

Before I go on, I would like to tell you how we came across this unexpected tidbit about their product implementation. It came up while we were performing a routine risk assessment, which in our case* is a little different than what most people consider risk assessments to be like. In our approach, we do not look for technical faults such as system vulnerabilities. The reason is simply that we do not consider such information to be particularly useful or interesting in the context of a risk assessment. In most organizations, there are usually plenty of risk mitigation processes for these types of issues, such as the handling of missing patches. Examples of such processes include monthly vulnerability scanning and penetration tests, along with many others. Most operations departments are fairly well trained in dealing with these once they are implemented, and so a risk assessment may wish

---

* Meaning at EAmmune, its clients, or any other place in which I have managed a security department ... which can, perhaps uncomfortably, be best described as "lots of places".

to note whether these processes are in place or not, or whether they are followed with a reasonable degree of adherence.

Unfortunately, so many risk assessments fail to stop there, and instead start incorporating the findings from these technical audit processes themselves into the assessment, thereby immediately diluting its effectiveness. The reason for this is simple: the human reality is that unless you manage these kinds of risk processes as part of your day job, they are otherwise completely uninteresting and irrelevant to you.

We consciously avoid that.

The one big thing we concentrate on instead is interviewing people and trying to get their idea of potentially risky practices and hidden, unpleasant realities within the company's operating environment. This follows from my belief that every company, collectively, *knows every risk there is to know about itself.* You just have to figure out who to talk to, and what to ask them. In other words, there is nothing that we can "discover" in a risk assessment that would actually be material new information, that is, something that nobody in the company knows about already.

A technically oriented "risk assessment" will not "discover" all the things that are wrong with an organization's security posture, since at the end of the day, it is merely a repackaging of other technical processes, as noted above; even if you have the best tools in the world all running for you inside all of your environments, the most you will get is a lopsided view of risk. That is, your view will be one that fully ignores people and their behaviors, as well as business processes and their impact on decision making, and similar "minor trivia".

But if we speak to the right cross-section of stakeholders within the organization, and if we know how to do so effectively, then we will end up with a really good picture of where the bodies are really buried and where the risks truly exist. And so it was in this case; we were chatting with various folks as part of our risk assessment, running some interviews. And it was one of the engineers who first clued us in that there might be a slight problem.

Amusingly, he brought it up as a shining, to him, example of how they were working to increase security, and from his perspective, he was entirely in the right to feel proud. What he said was that they had implemented a project for encryption within the tool, which led to securing all communications. He then, proudly, mentioned that they had "improved" the encryption so that it worked better for them, solving a performance challenge while still maintaining security.

We did not know to search for this issue, of course, but it was practically inevitable* that if we spoke to a long-time engineer in the company, this would have come up because encryption is, of course, a big part of security, and *everybody knows it*. All you had to ask was "give us an example or two of things going right", and it came out. I mean, how could it fail to come up? Here was a tricky obstacle that required engineering cleverness to solve, and their solution served as a cornerstone for resolving the biggest security headache they used to have.

Well, we are not software developers. We are security people, and as you might imagine, upon hearing this little gem our ears done got perked again.

We started going down the route of trying to understand what exactly it meant, that they had "improved the performance of the encryption algorithm". And that was when we discovered something that was actually pretty shocking.

First of all, what sort of encryption did they choose to use? They went with Advanced Encryption Standard (AES). That was a sensible choice, both for performance and for security reasons, and AES is of course a well known, respected, and wildly used encryption algorithm. It might have been the right one to use in this kind of implementation; I really have no idea, as I am not a crypto expert. What I do know is that due to performance reasons, they chose to use 128-bit encryption, which is maybe not as strong as 192 or 256 bits, but certainly is good enough – and it runs faster. And what do you know, it worked just fine.

It just did not work well *enough*.

Going to 128 bits did not quite solve the performance issue they were facing in the way that they had hoped it would. But it would have been really complicated to undo all the integrations and research and development to replace AES, so in thinking through this and trying to figure out how to optimize their algorithm, they came upon a solution.

Here we go.

---

* Really, I mean it. This never fails.

Ready?

The solution they settled on was to reduce the number of rounds that AES was using as part of the encryption process.

Now look, this is not a technical book, so I am not going to spend any time explaining how encryption works or how AES does its magic. But let me share just enough so that you have the necessary background to understand the impact of this sort of decision.

AES is what is called a block cipher. What it means, in plain terms, is that AES will take your message* that you are trying to encrypt, break it down into "blocks" of a certain size (in our case, 128 bits, or 16 computer "words"), and then apply a set of mathematical functions to convert that into another block of scrambled text. It will continue to do so repeatedly over a series of such transformations, also called *rounds*, until it finally rests. The final block of text (also 128 bits in size) is the corresponding encrypted message.†

Critically, the number of rounds being used is essential to the strength of the encryption algorithm. You can attack AES by various methods to try and break the encryption,‡ but it is generally considered secure if you use a sufficient number of rounds. Conversely, if the mathematical functions involved are not repeated enough times as part of the process – if there aren't enough rounds – then the strength of the resulting encryption becomes subject to those attacks.

However, as you can imagine, each such mathematical transformation takes a bit of time to go through. It causes a delay, in the form of that encryption performance tax we talked about earlier. As a side note, this is still an issue even today, years later, most commonly in high-performance database applications.

So now that you have a rudimentary background, let's get back to our story: what the engineers who implemented AES in the communications tool decided to do in order to improve the performance of their encryption was to reduce the number of rounds.

My hope is that by now, this moment is exactly where your jaws would be dropping to the ground. It gets better: they actually tore

---

* Known as the "plaintext".
† Known, appropriately enough, as the "ciphertext".
‡ Such as "cryptanalysis" which I only tell you because it's a such cool term. Say it with me. Cryptanalysis. Cryptanalysis. Satisfying, isn't it?

down the algorithm and reduced the number of rounds from the recommended and "known secure" ten (for the 128-bit version of AES) and lopped off *eight of them*, leaving only two.

AES of course became extremely fast. It also became extremely vulnerable to attack. At only two rounds, I am told by people who know this stuff, it becomes practically trivial to break AES encryption.

We did not need to be crypto experts to figure out upon hearing it that this might, perhaps, not be the best way to solve the performance challenge.

Right.

Squaring our poor, hunched shoulders,* we went a-talkin' to a number of people in the organization, trying to explain this and that and what have you about what, in the context of this underpinning the security of the entire platform, we perceived as a fairly significant risk that needed a bit of priority attention. It did not take that long to speak to our executive sponsor and a couple more senior members of the engineering department.

That is when we came across the ever startling, no matter how many times we run across it, phenomenon colloquially known as "leave us alone, we know what we're doing".

It is practically our theme for this chapter. Remember the last story, where we provided actual proof of a serious vulnerability and a working exploit written by an actual crypto expert, and still ran into this phenomenon?

This was worse.

What we learned was that the idea for how they were implementing AES was based on input they received from a consultant that they had previously hired to help them find a method of securing their platform's communications.

Apparently, that consultant was the one who suggested that they use AES.

They insisted that the consultant, who was, in their words, a "Ph.D. in encryption" – to be honest, I am not entirely sure if I know what that means to this day, but that was how they described him – was the

---

* You're in Security for any length of time? Then your shoulders are poor. And hunched.

one who told them that to solve the performance problem, the easiest way to do so was to reduce the number of rounds in AES.

They trusted the fellow, and followed his advice. They had also paid him a good sum of money to help them come up with a solution, and they were not about to change their minds just because a bunch of idiots like us, that is, non-"encryption Ph.Ds", suggested that this might not be an ideal implementation.*

When you think about it, I can imagine this as a sort of miscommunication that happens sometimes. Right? It is entirely possible that somebody who does know what they are doing would say, in a theoretical sense, "sure, you can make things go faster by reducing the number of rounds"; it is undeniable that the performance of AES is improved as you reduce the number of rounds. It might well have been said with a hint of irony, and they might usually add something like "of course, you're also significantly weakening the algorithm when you do so" to that sentence. Yet it is entirely conceivable that the second part of the statement simply did not register because the person listening to you heard the first half and got excited.

Sounds implausible? And yet, that is exactly the sort of thing that you see happening everywhere, all the time, and usually with minor impact at worst. The reality in this particular case was that weak encryption ended up protecting everything, the entire platform and everything on it – including transactional details (and, yes, credit card and other sensitive account numbers).

AES encryption was the critical safety mechanism for this tool, and it simply was not implemented securely.

Another problem we faced in this instance was that unlike in the last story, this was not a very large company. It was not a Fortune-500. It was not about to authorize us to spend tens of thousands of dollars on bringing in a crypto expert to break the encryption mechanism to prove that it was designed incorrectly. And so it ended up being that no matter how much this appeared like a pretty significant risk for the company, they just were not going to fix it.

---

* At this point, you might raise an obvious objection: what if they were right? Sure, it's possible, but I did speak to a couple of crypto experts and shared the implementation details and they both shook their heads in that sad way that we all know and oh, so cherish.

I mean, why should they? They paid for advice from an expert, and it sure looked like it worked just fine to the naked eye. The communications definitely looked encrypted. They even had a couple of senior engineers show it to us on the screen, proudly pointing out the fact that ciphertext, not clear text, was clearly flowing through the pipe, if you will, between the communicating parties.

And yes, this made the solution, essentially and ironically, a "security by obscurity" type of control.* Go ahead, laugh. And after you are done, let me tell you that the next time you deal with one of the pompous types that tells you that "security by obscurity" does not work, for every one of those people I can recall ten stories like this one showing that it clearly *does* work for the people involved. Not because such controls work in a technical sense – they do not – but because they do work in a human sense. There is no question that anyone with the right skill set and an inclination to break these guys' encryption scheme could easily do so; but such a somebody would also have to decide to spend the effort on the endeavor, and most likely have to be pointed at it at least vaguely to know that it is an avenue worth pursuing. And it is in that latter bit that the "obscurity" portion ends up legitimately working in real life.

At least for a while.

Until it stops working.

I cannot tell you whether or not there was a happy ending to this story. The company kept growing after that, and then got acquired, and staff changed, and it is very unlikely that anyone ever revisited the issue. It is likely that this decision never bit them in the ass, which is the fundamental reality with information security: the vast majority of your bad security decisions will never manifest in actual negative outcomes.

If you ever wondered, chief, why security is such a difficult field to wrap your head around, that right there is a huge reason.

As an amusing footnote to this story,† it is probably worth pointing out that since the encryption implemented in this platform was so

---

* Meaning, in layman's terms, a control that serves its purpose simply by trying to "hide" something sensitive without really protecting it, and hoping that nobody notices.

† Other than the rest of the adoringly amusing footnotes in this book, of course.

poor as to be effectively worthless as a technical control, one might cynically suggest* that going down from two rounds to one would have served the same purpose, and gained even more performance.

After all, it would appear to be just as obscure.

***

While both of these stories involve encryption, that is obviously not the only area in which software development and security intersect in some potentially dramatic ways. Two other rather visible ones are access control, and logging and auditing, which are highly related to each other, and usually never really considered by development teams unless they have a security minded person present during the design phase. It may seem like a quaint question until you consider this: why *should* a developer writing code for a product think it is important to spend the (significant) effort on developing a well designed mechanism for *tracking themselves*? Of course they would not do that, if it even occurs to them, which unless they have been there before, it would not. From their perspective, it can be easily summarized thusly:

What a waste of time!

The story in Chapter 2, about the "big red button" library, is an example of a third such area – being privacy – which is growing rapidly, and also an example of how it should be handled. That is, at least, until legal got involved with that screwball mandate. A few years later we had the opportunity to make the same recommendation to a different customer, and with privacy regulations having advanced dramatically by that point, the wisdom of ensuring that every Personally Identifiable Information (PII) data element and record maintained and carried its own set of identifier tags across their vast data warehousing facility such that they could always easily locate and remove it if necessary was obvious. By this time the idea of serving a "user access rights request" – the right enshrined within the General Data Protection Regulation (GDPR†) allowing everyone to demand that a company delete all their personal data from the company's systems – all of that was well understood and accepted as a reality of business.

---

* OK, one might have actually suggested.
† The EU data privacy rule that has taken the world by storm.

What was perhaps a tad fascinating to me personally was that we still had to both suggest that they design the new data architecture this way, and explain how it should work; even though the concept itself was internalized, the data architecture team had not really considered the applicability of it to their design. It reflects the same underlying issue, which is that you cannot count on engineering teams to "think security" without extensive training, and certainly not because you wrote it in a policy. The basic reality is that engineers are trained to think in terms of "how (to make) things work", whereas security requires you to think primarily in terms of "how (to make) things break". The neural grooves, if you will, of these two lines of thinking are fundamentally different, and mastering both at once requires insight, experience, and a significant body of knowledge. Building this kind of discipline within an engineering organization must also take into account management hierarchies, turnover, and in the case of a software development shop (especially in a cloud services company), constant sales pressure, which is why it simply does not happen all that often.

**

"Sure", I can hear you thinking right now, "fine, for all your big talk, Barak, you still gave us a couple of examples here, and surprise surprise, they're both about encryption. You admit that encryption is hard. So it's not that much of a surprise when engineering teams might screw it up, regardless of good intentions", which would be a fair argument to make.

I shared these encryption examples because they are so easy to explain, illustrative of the kind of simple yet erroneous decisions that people make in engineering (especially in cloud environments) all the time. Routine decisions that are commonly made and yet to which we do not pay much attention are the ones that provide the foundation for so much of this new technology world we live in. And in the cloud, where all the control domains and boundaries are fuzzy, it is so much easier to trip up. It is in this very world where it is never entirely clear who owns what, and where people make so many hidden assumptions that it can be hard to, in layman's terms, know what's what.

For example, does your own Amazon Web Services (AWS) cloud account residing in its own Virtual Private Cloud (VPC*) mean you actually have full control of the encrypted data residing inside of that VPC? We can test this assumption, and it does not take long to realize it fails. For one thing, the AWS "invisible NOC†" – the folks running the network infrastructure at AWS – control the Hypervisors‡ … which means that they can at any time observe all the traffic running inside of those hypervisors … including, yes, encryption keys, if they choose to do so. The truth is that we merely assume that they will be doing a good job and not acting maliciously, and it is a reasonable assumption to make. Plus AWS has deep pockets so if something does go wrong because one of their employees turned rogue, they could cover the damages.

Still, if we are to be honest with ourselves, that is all it is.

An assumption.

And yes, you can try to implement all sorts of controls to account for this, too, but they are both expensive and complicated, and the reality is, most private companies that live in the cloud do not, including large scale Software as a Service (SaaS) vendors that count many large enterprise customers as clients. In fact, because we all realize that this is the reality, this assumption is baked into security questionnaires – the "invisible NOC" question rarely if ever gets asked, because what would be the point of asking? We know what the answer will be. We just accept that AWS (or Google Cloud Platform, or Microsoft Azure) is safe and move on.

It becomes a hidden assumption, a forgotten one.

Let us get back to everyday engineering decisions, though, because that is the focus of this chapter. I would like to share another example from a few years ago, from another company with which I was involved. The decision they made is going to sound outrageous. Yet

---

* Essentially an imagined boundary between your virtual systems and anyone else's, so that even though everyone is sharing the same underlying hardware computing resources, their computations and data don't intermingle. It *usually* works.

† This stands for "Network Operations Center".

‡ The software that controls all this impressive virtualization, that is, the transformation of large-scale physical computing devices into an infinite number of virtual computing "bubbles" that everyone can share without sharing – see VPC above.

I promise you that this kind of decision is replicated in many places, even when we all feel like there is today a much greater appreciation for and awareness of the impact of bad security decisions.

They still do not teach security as an essential component in most computer science courses, after all.

I was asked at the time to come in and look into the company's payment card industry (PCI) compliance environment,* following an internal realization that they needed to become compliant in order to continue to serve their customer base. They wanted to figure out what it would take, and after providing the company with that initial assessment, hired me to help manage the security program.

A little while later, they hired a fellow who became their internal head of security, and had me supporting him. Let's call him Cole. One of the things that we were doing together on a continuing basis was investigating the environment to find unidentified areas of concern. Every time something ... funny† ... came up, we would take these wonderful walks along the adjoining waterway or in the streets of the lovely town where the company was located, and discuss these issues. This approach had multiple benefits, including better fitness for us as well as being away from the office and in an environment where we could not be easily overheard, let alone understood by any casual observer.

Cole and I built a friendship out of these walks which lasts to this day, and he is another one of my favorite people in the security world. His acerbic wit, combined with a natural gift for storytelling that rivals the best, make him a terrific person to discuss pretty much anything with, let alone the kind of crazy that we regularly encounter in our field.

To top it all off, we also instituted an admittedly awfully inappropriate mechanism we called "Speak with a Foreign Accent Day" (SFAD), which we triggered during those times when the insanity seemed too real. From the moment one of us declared it an SFAD day, and the choice of accent (Italian, French, Russian, and German were fairly popular), we spent the rest of the day speaking to each

---

* Aren't I so lucky with this PCI business?
† In security-speak, this translates to "a routine 5-alarm fire".

other (and occasionally others who were in on it, like the company's jovial general counsel) in that accent.

What can I say? It is a stressful field, security.

You do what you can to survive.

While not entirely relevant to the story, I can assure you that it was an SFAD day ... and a multiaccented one, at that.

Before I proceed, I would point out that the story highlights an interesting problem in the compliance world, and provides an insight into how much compliance is dependent on the people reporting the information to the auditor. There is recognition of that in financial audits, and regulatory controls with enforcement teeth behind them placed to ensure that companies aren't cooking the books. No such thing exists in the security world. Enforcement is generally achieved via commercial obligations in contracts, and on the rare occasion that something bad happens, lawyers and financial settlements.

So what happened?

Like many other companies with a sensitive database that supported a large "live" (24 × 7 × 365) environment, this one had an engineering support team – the database administration (DBA) group – that was working constantly to maintain it and fix problems, scale up the system, and develop new ways to organize data more efficiently. Much of this work was happening during "on-call" (off) hours, when people not in the office were working from home, logging in remotely in order to provide the support that was necessary to keep the company growing.

So far, so good. Where, then, does this turn, well, funny?

It all started with an apparently routine decision that someone had to make. A small one, nothing earth-shattering. Kind of ho-hum, really. See, the DBAs were getting increasingly irritated at some point because there was a bit of an additional burden to logging in remotely and going through the gates we had implemented in order to keep their production environment at least somewhat secure. Basic stuff, really, like using a Virtual Private Network (VPN) client to authenticate to a bastion jump host,* and then having to separately log in to the database itself.†

---

* In non-technical terms, establishing a secure connection to a secure host that served as the "doorway" to the rest of the systems, like a security checkpoint at the airport.
† Multi-factor authentication was still in its infancy, so none of that. Like I said, simple.

Sounds familiar? This is a very common setup.

Still, after a while some of the senior on-call staff decided that they had sort of had enough of that. It was annoying to have to authenticate every time, for one thing. They were doing a lot of work to support the company through a period of rapid growth, which made it important to accomplish tasks quickly; the pressure was on. Security, as it often does in these situations, was at best an afterthought.

So they made a decision.

They opened their big database to the public Internet directly.

Yes, what you just read is exactly right. If you knew where to look you could direct your SQL* query directly to the internal database, right through ports 1523 and 1524,† from the public Internet and execute those queries, as long as you were authenticated. The way we even came across this was completely accidental. I was chatting with one of the engineers and it came up as we were talking about how they were supporting the system from home during those off hours.

He actually mentioned it offhandedly, as in "yeah, it was kind of annoying and slowing us down to have to do the whole VPN thing, so we solved it this way". He went on to explain that they had to do something to deal with the problem we Infosec people introduced, that is, that we forced them to authenticate remotely to a VPN jump host and then authenticate to the database internally, so they could work from home. They felt that we created too many barriers that way, and that it "wasn't like working from the office".

What he meant by that was that in the office they had something called a site to site to VPN tunnel set up. So the extra authentication steps were not necessary because being logged in at the office was considered to already be in an internal, safe environment. This used to be, at that time, a fairly normal setup in a lot of organizations. Contextually, this was before cloud computing became extremely popular, meaning that this was all based on running their own infrastructure in their own data center. They just wanted to make working from home feel the same as being in the office.

And who could blame them?

Really, it did not sound outrageous to them. They still had to authenticate and, as the engineer explained to me, you had to know

---

* That's the name of a common database "language".

† The computer communications channel for database queries of this nature.

the Internet address of the database to even know that it was there ... remember the "security by obscurity" discussion? In this case, it combined classically with engineering training, that is, the expectation that things will work as designed. In that fictional context, they were sort of right; assuming there was no way to mess with the database with malicious, malformed requests, and assuming authentication worked properly, and that malicious parties could not find the database address on the public Internet, then there would be no additional risk ...

As you might imagine, Cole and I had a rather, uhh, amusing conversation (in "French") the following morning as we were walking by the river.

We did, of course, close this hole, although as is sadly too often the case, it took some internal arguing to convince the team that it was necessary.

Why am I bringing up this story? Surely this was a rare case, and even if not, that sort of thing does not happen anymore. People are smarter about security now. Nobody would ever do this today. Right?

Right. Of course.

In reality, even today, cloud storage systems like AWS S3 are often set up badly and cause sensitive data leaks.* A common error is setting them up as open to the world, with the only thing hiding them being the long string of characters that you need to access them, which is roughly equivalent to knowing what the IP is of the target system in the example above. If you have that address represented by that string of characters, then you can point your favorite data acquisition tool at it and gain access to the storage system and everything stored within it.

And that is without counting more nuanced engineering decisions such as "failing open" when parts of the authentication system stop working for whatever reason, even as the underlying information may be very private or even sensitive. As a current example at the time of writing this chapter, just look at what happened to the application Parler in January of 2021, and how its users' sensitive information leaked due to this engineering decision and its aftermath following

---

* For your personal amusement, run a Google search for something like "aws s3 bucket breaches", sit back with a cup of your favorite beverage, and enjoy.

the events on the day of congressional certification of the electoral vote in the 2020 United States presidential election.*

It happens.

Regularly.

---

* It's worth looking up, but in a nutshell, political tides caused the site's third party used for high-security authentication to suspend services, which when combined with the decision to "fail open" – that is, continue working if that integration failed – and poor site code, allowed a hacker to create an administrator account for themselves and, well, go from there.

5

ADVICE FROM EXPERTS

Those stories were fun, but they all were the result of security decisions by software engineers inexperienced with security. So am I implying that the people with the erroneous thinking are always from the ranks of developers?

Of course not. It is just that the inevitable result of the intersection between Infosec and software development is simply that there are a lot of stories in that particular arena.

Lest you think that I hesitate to point the finger at our own crew, if you will, let me share some stories about security people screwing up, often by providing the wrong guidance. One thing that goes without saying when security people give the wrong guidance about security is that unlike pretty much anybody else doing that, security people generally cannot hide behind the supposed complexity of the discipline when, well, ...

... when they screw up security.

It is, after all, their domain of expertise.

Security is the foundation of the job they are hired to do. They are there to give good security advice. They might well be wrong – we all make mistakes, after all – but the character of any such mistake should, in theory at least, be less misinformed or perhaps more nuanced. Sadly, because of the nature of the field, the impact of bad security decisions can sometimes be heightened.

Thus the stories in this chapter, and why I chose to have a chapter with such stories in the first place, all share the added benefit of being exceptionally delicious (or dubious, or horrifying), regardless of the end result; because, as we have discussed previously, most of our otherwise bad security decisions do not come back to bite us in the patootie.

Let us start with one that did turn out badly, and resulted in significant losses. Let us talk about one case involving a financial institution.

DOI: 10.1201/9781003133308-6

Right. A retail bank.

See, banks are a little special in the security context because banks are arguably a type of institution where the stakes are highest. At least as far as consumers are concerned, if somebody hacks your Facebook account and posts some silly stuff in your name, you are not usually going to be materially harmed (want to know what is Facebook's greatest liability shield? It is, simply, that one fact). It is hard to prove large damages from such an event. Clearly, there are exceptions, such as if you happen to be a public figure reliant on social media. But for most people, the kind of harm involved might be limited to, say, embarrassment, discomfort, or simply the pain in the ass effort of having to recover access to your hacked account.

Facebook themselves sure aren't super helpful there, either.

However, if somebody takes over your bank account and liquidates it, then it is very easy to quantify the damages, as they are equal to your previous bank balance. And the harm can be very, very real as people who have had this happen to them have experienced. It could mean that your life savings are gone, or that suddenly your bills bounce and you start going down a never-ending downwards loop of a tarnished credit record, which can lead to an inability to rent or apply for a job or get healthcare* or a host of other bad to terrible outcomes. If your bank account is emptied by a nefarious actor, it is also often difficult to recover those funds. It takes an investigation because the banks are generally not happy about having to fund such a loss.† And that takes time, which some may not have if they are dependent on that account for their daily expenses.

In other words, it can get pretty messy pretty quickly. There are also plenty of documented cases where a person's bank account was liquidated because of careless password choices, and while in the US the funds are typically ultimately restored, consumer protection laws may not exist or cover such losses depending on where you live.

---

* At least in the US ... and possibly similar third world (at least when it comes to healthcare) countries.

† It is maybe interesting to note that, at least in the US, the bank is considered the victim, rather than the consumer whose account was hacked.

Alright, so the consumer has to be better about protecting their account. But what happens when the guidance that the bank provides is in itself erroneous?

The example I have for you here is from a (non-US) bank that had undergone a brute force attack on its systems which resulted in an overall fair number of accounts being compromised and dollars being lost. I want to share this particular story not because it ultimately caused the bank a material loss – yes, losses (in the millions) were incurred, but they were limited enough that the bank was able to recover from them more or less without a hitch. Rather, it is because of the way in which their outsourced security experts chose to set up the arrangement of consumer passwords to the bank's website, which ended up playing a part in the overall success of the subsequent attack. Specifically, they made a couple of implementation choices that might not sound that unusual to a layman. Yet they were ultimately terrible security advice.

So what did they do? Well, the first of those bad choices was easily observable when you attempted to create a login for online access to your bank account(s).

See, when you tried to create a password for your new account, you would be shown a mostly standard list of requirements for password construction. Many of them are going to be very familiar to anyone who has ever interacted with any site online in (at least) the past decade: you have to pick a password that includes CAPITAL letters and small letters, as well as numbers. The password also had to be of a certain minimum size. In this case, because this was a while ago and such limitations were still somewhat common, the password also had a maximum size, which the site happily informed you about.*

Before I continue the story, I would like to take a small detour into the somewhat interesting history of this particular aspect of password generation, referring in this case to the complexity requirement. That whole mumbo-jumbo about having capital letters and small letters and numbers and special characters is not necessarily a result of good security standards. Rather, it originated as a compromise, a mitigating factor against brute force attacks due to historical limitations in the

---

* Strike one. Telling an attacker how to limit the search space for potential password matches is never a good idea.

capacity of certain systems to store long passwords. To explain this in an intentionally simplified way, think of a system that is, say, limited to passwords of eight characters (a common field size) in length due to storage (in the sense of a database, not disk space) or other software limitations. The problem with that is that an eight-character limit also in turn limits the search space – that is, the overall total number of possible permutations that can possibly be constructed within that limit. You can create only that many eight-character passwords, after all. It therefore stands to reason that a brute force attack – one that attempts to iterate through all the possibilities until it finds the correct one – has a much greater chance of success when executed against a more limited search space.

The attack will conclude the algorithmic analysis faster.

Now comes the interesting bit: the recognition that most humans are also inherently lazy. This is not a criticism; all of us hate complex passwords at least a little bit, and plenty of treatises have been written about this topic and the tendency of humans to write these difficult to remember passwords on sticky notes.* Thus, it is not unfair to assume that in any system, the majority of users will *select the simplest form of password they can get away with*.†

And what would that be?

Why, all small letters (or numbers), of course.

"12345678" was for a fair while the most popular password used by people on the interwebs, for this exact reason.

Any good hacker takes advantage of such behavioral tendencies, and so they would configure their tools to first search through the permutations that only contain, say, numbers, dramatically narrowing down the search space even further; there are only ten digits to choose from, after all, and if you do not have to include letters (another 26) then your job of trying to crack some of the passwords becomes a whole lot easier, computationally speaking.

One way to ensure that the search space is larger and to compensate for that upper cap on the number of characters is, then, to do so by requiring complexity in password construction. That ensures that

---

* Memorably, and recently, in the screen adaptation of *Ready Player One*.
† Maybe I should call this "Barak's first rule of user access" and see what happens. Are you listening, world? I want a rule named after me.

each individual password cannot be cracked without iterating through a much larger set of possible constructions. However, note (and this is the important bit I am trying to get to for the purposes of our story when I finally get back to it) that there is a trade-off involved, in the sense that the password cracking tool, in knowing that complexity is required, can be configured from the outset to safely ignore all the permutations that do not include at least one character from each category. In other words, enforcing complexity both increases *and* decreases the search space at the same time – it just does much more of the former and much less of the latter.

So that is roughly where this whole complexity business comes from. The reality is that password length is generally a far better defense against automated password cracking than complexity can ever claim to be, since each new character raises the total number of possibilities exponentially. Put simply, a completely random, complex password that is eight characters long is always going to be less resistant to a pure brute force attack than pretty much any password that is, say, ten characters in length, even if the latter does not enforce complexity. This is especially true if there are no discernible upper limits on password length, as is true for any properly configured modern access control system. The reason for that is that hashing, the preferred method of storing passwords, ultimately produces a fixed-length stored value (in the form of a hash) for each password regardless of its original size – but I will avoid explaining that here, or discuss dictionaries and rainbow tables, or why at some point (beyond roughly ten characters) length also becomes irrelevant, or why passwords in general are simply not a great access control mechanism in the first place, or any number of other factors, as I would rather you stay awake.

Plus there are plenty of other books for that stuff.

We do stories here.

Ultimately, if you want to create good, strong passwords, even if you also have to make them complex, the best suggestion is to simply adopt common language phrases (also known as "pass phrases"). They would tend to be both long, and with the side benefit of being complex. Here are some increasingly facetious examples in English:

This is a good password.
This is a good password!

Is this a good password?
A good password, this is
A password; this is good

Notice that not only did I restrict myself to the same five words, I also used a different special character in each version, to boot.

Where is my gold star?

Anyway, let's get back from our detour and into our main narrative.

What was particularly interesting about this bank's website – and again, keep in mind that this was an implementation by those highly paid security consultants, who were paid hefty sums to develop this system – was one additional requirement for safe password construction.

You could not have a password where the same character repeated more than twice in succession.

For example, the word "good" would work, but something like "ooohlalah" would not. The site would flag the three "o"'s and force you to come up with something else.

That requirement would certainly guarantee that any chosen passwords appeared to be more complex to any human looking at them.

Isn't that lovely?

If you are not rolling your eyes by now, let me point you a couple of pages back where we discussed the issue of limiting the search space. Password cracking is not done by humans laboriously trying out one password at a time, eyeing a spreadsheet. It is performed by soulless machines who do not get tired, just take time to try everything out, and do not "see" patterns the way humans see them.* And by setting this restrictive parameter, the number of possible passwords, and therefore combinations to test against, was reduced fairly dramatically, making the job of the password cracker a fair bit easier.

But that wasn't all.

The other bad thing they did was encrypt the passwords, instead of hash them.

Let us see if we can get through this one quickly (and you may recall the discussion from the previous chapter): passwords have only

---

* Computers generally suck at pattern detection, or at least they used to before artificial intelligence became a big deal.

one purpose, which is to allow a human to identify themselves to a computer in order to pass through a virtual gate. The computer has to store all the passwords of the various people allowed through that gate in order to match them against the passwords those people enter at the gate. In reality, though, the computer does not actually need to have the passwords themselves stored; it can rely on a mathematical derivation of them, which is called a hash. Hashes have unique properties, in particular the fact that they only work in one direction; once you hash a password, the resulting garbled text cannot be reverted back to the original password,* even though each password will always produce the same garbled text. By storing password hashes, the computer can still validate identities – when someone provides their password, the computer simply hashes it and matches the resulting value with the stored hash for that user – without running the risk of all those passwords being stolen. Even if someone did get their hands on the stored hashes, they could not extract the original passwords from them.

Encryption, on the other hand, is bi-directional. Something that was encrypted can later be decrypted with the appropriate key. This is very useful for exchanging secret messages, but why would you ever want to decrypt a password?

Let alone a whole bunch of them?

For online access to a *bank*?

By the way, some time after I got exposed to this story, I did in fact learn the reasoning behind this oddball choice. Would you believe that the bank insisted it was good customer service to be able to tell their technology-challenged users, over the phone, what their passwords were, in the unfortunate case that they lost them?

Indeed.

Customer service at its finest.

Ultimately, what you think happened did, in fact, end up happening. They lost (one of) the encrypted password file(s).

To their credit, they realized this happened fairly quickly, and by the time the thief cracked the entire password list – a process that was helped by the limitations on password construction they had implemented, combined with the fact that the passwords were

---

* Yes, I realize that we discussed exactly how this *can* happen in the last chapter; I mean in the case where hashing is properly implemented.

encrypted (with the same key) instead of hashed – they got a fair number of those stolen passwords rotated, and placed additional limitations on transactions through their website. The damages totaled, perhaps, a few million dollars in all, something they could well handle.

But talk about self-inflicted wounds!

***

At least there is no way that this sort of thing was going to happen today, right? Surely this story, which admittedly took place more than a decade ago, and in a foreign country, could not possibly happen here and now?

Right.

I present to you a circa 2020 Fortune-500 bank's* password construction advice, directly from their website:

Your Passcode must

✔ Be 8 to 20 characters

✔ Use at least 1 upper case letter, 1 lower case letter, and 1 number

✔ Not repeat the same number or letter more than 3 times in a row

✔ Not contain spaces, and may only use these characters
  @ # * ( ) + = { } / ? ~ ; , . - _

You know what's good about this? The minimum password length.

You know what's bad about this? Practically everything else.

Forget all the other stuff … just tell me why on earth, for the love of all that is holy, would you *not allow people to use spaces*? The most effective way to construct strong passwords is – all together now – by encouraging the use of pass phrases. Pass phrases quite literally depend on the use of spaces.

What is wrong with these people?[†]

In 2020!

---

* Oh, I am dying so hard to name and shame here, but the fear of upsetting this kind of organization stays my hand.

† I just can't hold it in anymore. It was Bank of America.

***

I suppose you may now be wondering "if I can't even trust security people with this stuff ... where can I turn?", and that would be a fairly valid concern.

Remember what happened in the dotcom bubble days? Circa 1997 or so, everyone's* resume suddenly started sporting a new bullet, something along the lines of "web developer" or even, simply, "HTML". Whether they actually had actual knowledge in web development, let alone legitimate, real experience in the field, was secondary to the job at hand, which was to get one of them fancy new high-paying jobs in web development.

And because so few employers had any clue about hiring these folks, a lot of people got into roles they were generally not qualified for, and learned on the job. The "fake it til you make it" mantra made an excellent showing as the fever pitch around these newfangled Internet companies had its dials turned to 11 and the millennium drew to a close.

Well, these days security is about as hot as web development was back then, and suffers from similar issues, that is, it has the following three traits in common:

1) most people do not understand it; and
2) employers know they need it; and
3) everyone fears it.

It makes for a potent, explosive psychological cocktail and can lead to dramatic results. There are plenty of people walking around already with fancy titles like "Chief Information Security Officer (CISO)" that have very little idea of what the role is truly about or how to perform it without pissing everybody off.

Oh, don't look at me with that shocked face. You know it's true.

The worst part of it is that some of the more skilled ones, the ones that have gotten the title at some point along the way and actually managed to construct new careers around it, are now in real leadership positions in some very large organizations, but still without ever having gotten the training or experience on the business side. This has

---

* Or at least everyone who was tuned in to the times – which was most everybody.

knock-on effects as others that are not in Security struggle to make sense of the discipline and try their best to adjust.

I recall having a fairly long conversation with a senior partner at a venture capital firm who was trying to construct some methodology around security for their portfolio companies, and he asked me what seemed like a simple question.

"Barak", he started, "you have all this experience with CEOs and boards ... can you give me a slide you use to communicate security to the board?"

I knew where he was headed, and I took a deep breath before answering.

"I can give you examples while removing the identifying details, if you like, but they are contextual so there is no template to it". I knew he would not be satisfied.

"No, I get that it's contextual, but I want the one slide format – whatever you use for these", he said again.

"Alright. But again – it's generally just three to four bullets", I responded.

"But how do you communicate progress?" He sounded a bit surprised. "What metrics do you use?"

Finally, I had him.

"I don't".

"Huh?" The surprise became palpable.

"I don't use metrics. It makes no sense to do so, unless you insist on treating Security as a technology discipline which you can measure in vulnerabilities and attack vectors". I waited a few seconds to let him digest this.

"Look", I added. "When, say, chief counsel presents to a board, they don't give them tables with metrics, do they? It wouldn't make sense. They would provide the necessary, contextual information to support decision making, but they are not going to measure their performance by how many contracts they worked through. And if they did, board members will surely not actually care about it. It's a level of detail they don't need to do their job as board members. Right?"

"Riiiiight", he said, hesitantly.

"The same goes for security. Sure, we deal with these things as part of our job, but it's not interesting to a board. The only reason a CISO tells this stuff to a board is that they don't know how to communicate about the things that matter – what they are doing to support the business goals of the company – and this is one thing they do understand and have control over, so it makes them comfortable. Everybody smiles, they all check the 'informing the board about cyber risk' box, and move on with the business of the company, with neither side actually understanding each other. So … what's the point?"

He still looked unconvinced.

"Let me ask you this", I continued. "Why on earth should a board care how many security vulnerabilities are in a piece of software the company is developing? Isn't that the CISO's job to care about it and manage it? Why is this level of detail necessary for them? How does it help them do their job better? In what context? How can they even understand it? One thing I really dislike is this whole idea that the board doesn't listen to the CISO. The board listens alright. With the occasional exception, you don't normally get to be a board member for a large public firm by being stupid. It's just that we seem to insist on telling them dumb and irrelevant things, so they tune us out".

"OK, then do you have an example for me?" he asked. "Just so I see what you mean".

"Sure", I said. "Here is a recent one where I had to provide a board slide. Due to the pandemic, the business had suffered grievously, with all the attendant impact. It was struggling to survive. Before I tell you what I did say, do you agree that had I provided one of those metric laden slides, I'd have branded myself forever as a useful idiot with no business ever rising above the level of technologist?"

"Yeah, I can see that", he laughed.

"Cool. So here is what I did say. I first pointed out that actual cyber risk has fallen dramatically as well; not only because there was so much less activity on the platform, but primarily because any breach would have a much smaller impact due to the dramatically lowered level of activity. In other words, a hacker would have a lot less to steal, and as a result, breach associated costs – the actual thing that matters to a board – would be much smaller. That took all of one bullet".

He was beginning to grin on the Zoom.

"In my second bullet, I pointed out that at the new level of business activity, and the resulting skeleton workforce (they had to shrink by a staggering 80% or so as part of their survival strategy), the company was effectively operating at roughly the level of maybe a series C

Silicon Valley startup". I knew he could instantly relate to that, and it would help frame it in his mind.

Now his face was registering significant interest. I really did have him on the hook.

"For my third bullet, I suggested that, while the level of operations and business have been savaged, the market perception of the company in the public and regulators' eyes had remained roughly the same".

His eyes dilated as he made the neural connections, so I hastened to finish up before he did it for me.*

"And so I wrapped up with the last bullet stating that from my perspective as their CISO, the biggest risks I saw were associated with the mismatch between public perception and actual operations, and the likeliest area where they could manifest was in privacy,† where any class or regulatory action would assume legacy enterprise status, and the associated costs could be overwhelming as a result, unless the company was prepared in advance to help outside parties match expectations and reality".

"Which, amusingly enough, turned out to be what legal was going to tell them in the next slide, too", I finished.

"And what did you state as accomplishments and go forward suggestions?" he asked after a few seconds.

"Oh, that. I listed consolidation of expenditures, especially the removal of a large number of security tools and outsourcing of security operations, while providing support for a digital transformation effort that went on steroids since there was a lot less at risk from moving fast; simplification of the compliance posture; and pouring a lot more effort into the areas where the big residual risks were, namely legal and privacy, where I also suggested adding a little bit of investment into new evidence producing tools that would make handling any legal action related to privacy easier and cheaper".

"You literally listed killing off the security tools as an accomplishment? As the CISO?"

"Yes, of course", I said. "Why wouldn't I? If you trust me as the leader of the security organization, wouldn't you expect me to be

---

* Oh, vanity.
† For this company, the chief privacy officer was reporting to me.

sensitive to the operating environment of the business and adjust appropriately along with it?"

By then, he seemed to have forgotten the full context of the scenario, namely that I was not even employed by that company. I was just the vCISO.

***

The kind of unfortunately common but misguided thinking around security, this whole "guard at the gate" mentality, can often create significant hidden costs for multiple stakeholders as well.

Consider for a moment another very large firm where I spent several years advising their staff and leadership on security matters. In their case, there were some complications, including a security department that was the worst of all worlds: the in-house team that works for someone else.

What do I mean by that?

In this case, it would be a department that is in fact comprised of full-time employees, but is dedicated to a separate corporate owner and split amongst many constituents in the form of various subsidiaries.

Why do I say it is the worst of all worlds?

Because when you have an in-house team, with all the challenges that brings, at least those folks are in theory focused on your particular issues, and therefore have a higher likelihood of coming up with the right approaches over time. And since I brought it up: the challenges are that for most companies, there simply isn't a legitimate need for most kinds of full-time security staff (go ahead, quote me on that). Security is a highly specialized discipline, with many even more specialized sub-disciplines, and by the time you bring in people with expertise in each of these domains, you need a lot more activity to justify their positions than is typically legitimately required by any one of those positions. Ultimately, it creates a dissatisfying, demoralizing, and inefficient mismatch between the skills you pay for and how you can legitimately use them.

Fundamentally, this is the reason why I created my company, EAmmune. Which brings us to the outsourced model: your security program is managed by outsourced personnel that are not dedicated to you. In this case, your security staff is not comprised of full-time employees, which means that they are less in tune with that daily "vibe" in companies, especially younger and more dynamic ones. But in return for this lower engagement, you gain a tremendous benefit in terms of resource optimization; access to all the different types of specializations but only as you need them, paying only for the appropriate slice of this extremely expensive skill set and only when you actually need to utilize it. If your provider does a good job, they would have a method for continuing engagement at the program level to ensure that those necessary skills are made available at the right time, and also be training your internal staff along the way on how to incorporate the daily aspects of the security function into their individual positions.

To get back to this organization, the setup there basically mixed together the disadvantages in both models. Staff were full time, yes, but not for this subsidiary (or any other); their focus was never and could never be on this specific company, even though it was a highly profitable subsidiary in the corporate owner's portfolio. At the same time, because they formally had a "security department", everybody could pretend that security was a priority, even when it clearly was not treated that way in practice, and the result was as you would expect it to be: a hodgepodge of inconsistent, often conflicting internal controls, and very little oversight, resulting in an ineffective overall posture and a frankly breathtaking waste of resources, as different teams all did their best without any centralized coordination. You know how, in security, you can often skin the cat in twelve different ways?* This place was like a virtual trade show floor. You could be walking around seeing one widget, then turn the corner or go to the next floor, where you would see two other thingamabobs doing the same thing.

This contextual mismatch was made particularly acute, though, when it came to security for end users, where the corporate owners decided that what worked for them should work for everyone else, ensuring that employees and others working in these subsidiaries had to abide by policies made for an entirely different working environment – that of the owner. Which brings me to the amusing story of just how inane this all was, and also illustrates how damaging misaligned security can be to an organization, and not because it necessarily leads to a breach.

Productivity still counts, right?

---

* Sorry for the imagery. Cats are awesome. Plus the Internet is made of them.

As a consultant, I worked with these guys for years while never connecting to their network, so was not really exposed to this stuff. Signs were there; they had a guest wireless network that was ostensibly set up for the explicit purpose of allowing guests to use the Internet without having any access to internal networks. It did do that. However, in a classic example of someone taking security to the "next level" of irrationality,* they decided that their guests and their own corporate or personal devices using this guest network should be subject to various security scans and limitations, one of which was that Linux-based operating systems were categorically excluded from being granted access to this guest WiFi. I tried to find out once why that was the case, and apparently it was because their gateway tool could not scan my Linux laptop for anti-virus software, so in the interest of safety, I should not be allowed to browse my favorite porn sites, uhh, access my own company's Gmail account.

Then a year later they decided Gmail itself was not safe either so they blocked that, too. About that: did I mention they ran a Microsoft-based Exchange environment, with what one could define as severely unpatched domain controllers and Exchange servers?

I won't even go into the various implications of them scanning and potentially taking action (such as recording email traffic) on devices belonging to other corporations accessing their guest WiFi that was, remember, completely and successfully segregated from their own corporate WiFi. Typically the folks that would come in would be salespeople, so they would not know to complain. Nor will I go into the inevitable and, err, amusing conclusion that, apparently, in their minds Windows-based laptops were inherently more secure than Linux-based ones *when it came to malware*.

But I will point out, again as politely as I can, that as a consultant, I needed access to the Internet in order to perform the job that they hired me to do. Say they chose to send me an email with important information, and that information was not easily consumable by staring at a tiny phone screen; how was I to consume it? In a striking example of how bad security decisions create bad security outcomes, and especially after access to cloud email systems was blocked, I regularly witnessed employees storing documents on USB keys provided

---

* I wanted to say "stupidity" but am trying to stay polite. We'll see how long it lasts.

to them by vendors in order to share those files with the vendors in order to support the work that the vendors needed to do. And if anyone tells me that this is better than having those documents being sent as attachments to emails that end up in an enterprise Gmail account ... *

Anyway, thankfully we live in the age of technology and I was able to circumvent this particular bit of insanity for a good long while by using my phone as a wireless Internet gateway for my laptop. Since this was some years ago, performance was pretty slow, but certainly good enough to get email and keep up Yahoo Finance on the side to track my portfolio (we all have our vices). Ultimately, as a person whose hourly rates are rather hefty, my time may be considered fairly valuable, and I'll be damned if I waste any of it on this kind of nonsense.

But then, probably partly because I constantly made fun of these kinds of "security controls", yet could not be easily told to shut the door behind me on my way out,† the company decided to grant me my very own company laptop and internal user account.

∗∗∗

What, you thought the story was over?

No, my friends. We are only now getting to the good parts.

See, the first thing that I was confronted with by being allowed into the hallowed inner sanctum of their corporate WiFi network was, of course, the selection of a strong, secure password.

Remember all that discussion earlier in this chapter about passwords? I did not just do that to waste your time and fill this book with more words (although that is probably a nice side effect from my publisher's perspective). It was also to prepare you for having a better understanding of these guys' internal password standard, implementation, and enforcement.

Here is what their standard looked like: they required *extra*-complex passwords (see below), with no repeats of the last 12 passwords used

---

* I wanted to end with "I'd slap them upside the head", but I really, really am trying to stay polite.

† What can I say? I'm sorta cute that way.

(best practice typically calls for somewhere between four and six, so *clearly* more is better, right?*), and the PCI-influenced 90-day password rotations. So far, so (more or less) normal.

But guess at what minimum they set their password length?

16.

16 characters.

You know how difficult it is to set and remember complex passwords? Now do it with 16 characters.

So choose a pass phrase, you say? Not good enough for these guys. See, they did not count spaces as special characters, and they still insisted that each password included *all four categories* of small and capital letters, numbers and special characters, thereby making the use of pass phrases a lot more difficult than it ever needed to be. After all, remember from our previous discussion that the purpose of pass phrases is to allow a typical[†] user to create something they can easily remember, as a way to encourage length over complexity. But if you force both, the whole thing quickly collapses under its own weight.

The way that it collapses is simple and predictable; people start writing down their passwords on paper that they "hide" in their wallets or under their keyboards, or sometimes simply on a sticky note permanently stuck to the empty real estate present on either side of their laptop's touchpad. Oh, yes they do. They also quickly develop a strong resentment for security, which means that their natural inclination to not listen to security nor retain anything that security tells them is powerfully reinforced.

And to cap it all off, in a masterstroke of ingenuity I have yet to witness in this context in any other organization large or small, security in this organization came up with another important security control. They did what a lot of folks do, which is prohibit users to install software on their laptops, unless such software was preapproved on the company's internal app store.

Want to venture a guess which type of software was not present in the approved application list?

---

* Wrong. Just wanted to make sure I say it somewhere before someone jumps.
† All you technology woke folks, I'm not talking about you.

Let me give you a few seconds. I need to get a refill for my coffee cup anyway.

.

.

.

.

.

.

Got it?

You're right. There was not a single approved password vault* available. In fact, they were all forbidden because, I came to learn after a few weeks to trying desperately to understand the logic behind this decision, corporate security wanted to evaluate the security of each application themselves, and until they decided which one was good enough for them, none of them would be approved.

At least two years later, when I had last checked, they had still to approve one password vault, let alone actually suggest the idea to the workforce.

Thankfully, my personal favorite vault (Keepass) has a containerized version you can use without having to install anything, so I simply copied that over and at least had one for myself. I also showed this solution to others and several folks ended up using it as well, again illustrating how dumb the entire scheme was to begin with. But those were technologists. The vast majority of people in the company dealt with it in various ways, but with one common theme – they learned to mistrust Infosec and hate security with a bit of extra passion.

Take a breath, because believe it or not, we are not done yet.

Soon after I navigated this particular bit of ridiculousness, I came across a new security control: the network session expiration.

Security had apparently determined that a great threat to their operations was the possibility of rogue wireless devices connecting to their internal WiFi network, even after enforcing controls such as

---

* Those things that help you keep loads of complex long passwords without having to remember any of them, like Lastpass or 1Password.

those insane passwords, multi-factor requirements on every login, and device-based authentication.*

So they added certificate-based authorization as well. I mean, more security is always better, right? And in a way, they were right: it was very, very difficult to bypass all these controls and get on the internal WiFi network if you did not have the right device, with the right certificates, and the right accounts and multi-factor and all that jazz.

Here is the problem with this kind of approach: it also erects plenty of barriers in front of legitimate, authorized users.

See, in my role I only got to their offices once every week. The way their certificate authentication system worked, if the device was not present on the network when the "refresh cycle" or rollover of authentication occurred, then it would have to get all the certificates resigned.

Sounds pretty innocent, right?

Sure does.

Now let's get into the pragmatics.

The rollover happened every 24 hours.

The certificate resigning process was dependent on the ability to produce a proper handshake, which was disallowed by the other side of the authentication system which was waiting for an approval from the certificate side. The certificate side would not resign the certificates unless it got authorization from that other part ... which waited for the certificate part ... which waited for that other part ...

Employees usually did not feel this because they were at the office every day, and left their laptop there, or if they took it with them, when they got home, they would connect their laptops and sign on remotely, which would allow the certificates to be resigned anyway.

But if you were someone who only used their corporate issued laptop once a week, like me ... or, say, went on vacation and did not work while on said vacation (the horror!), or any number of reasons why the resigning could not occur on time ...

Your laptop would not reconnect. Sometimes it would if you waited long enough; I discovered after several weeks that it might happen

---

* That is, the system looked at the physical hardware address of the wireless network card upon connection, and if it wasn't previously registered (most commonly as in belonging to a laptop they owned), the connection would be denied.

randomly between 60 and 90 minutes in. Apparently one of the systems outwaited the other one in the background or something, probably an amusing race condition* that I never bothered to explore further.

I kid you not, on any given day, there were always a couple of people waiting at the IT help desk asking them to manually re-register their corporate-issued machines to the corporate network. I was in that line a couple of times myself until one of the engineers took me aside and showed me how they solved the problem for themselves: by dropping into the shell on boot, erasing the previous certificate, and then rebooting normally, the system would consider the laptop as newly issued, match the internal hardware address to its registration profile, and issue new certificates. The process took less than five minutes and was pretty simple to execute.

Read that last part again. The company's technically savvy internal users had to figure out a way to hack the company's own security controls because they otherwise were prevented from logging in to do their job!

It may sound quaint, but the big problem here is not just the irritation that this caused employees, but also lost productivity; all those people losing an hour here and there, or having to spend time at IT, with the IT people who had other things they had to do as well … every one of these mini-events caused the loss of hours of skilled labor.

And for what?

At best an extremely marginal benefit at the very edges of the security forest?

"Their security must have been pretty good", I can literally hear you thinking after this kind of story. But see, the reality is that it was actually pretty bad in plenty of much more important places. I will tell you about one in a second, but the point that I wish to illustrate with this is not just about security run amok, but also about why security cannot ever be successful if it is managed as a technology discipline: when you do it that way, your controls will tend to reflect the technology biases of your security leader. This means things will end up,

---

* In broad brush strokes, a "race condition" is when a security control fails because the timing of unrelated events within the same system creates an exposure that can be exploited.

at best, as uneven, and at worst, as total blind spots. Some areas will be great, others will suck, and from the perspective of whomever it is that is setting out to hurt you, it is always, inevitably going to be the weakest link that they would choose to go after.

And those parties,* by virtue of their expertise and inclination, tend to have a good eye for blind spots.

That proverbial caravan moves at the speed of its slowest vehicle.

And yes, this is true even for large, well-resourced security organizations, as was the case for this company. Which brings me to the example of how this issue manifested where it actually matters: inside their data center, in the beating heart of their technology operations.

One thing these folks did was process credit card transactions – a metric boatload of them. In a minor, yet unfortunately common implementation error of a token vault, theirs was installed in a single-channel configuration …

Wait. Hold on. What was that?†

Let's unpack this: the company used an outside service to store all credit card account numbers, instead of storing them locally on their own systems. That is a good idea, as it shifts the responsibility of handling that particular kind of sensitive data to a party (the "vault") that is usually better capable of managing it securely.

Instead of using live account numbers, the company uses made-up, fake numbers that look similar to credit card numbers but are completely meaningless should they be stolen. Each of these fake numbers is a reference to an actual account number in the vault, and they are called tokens – hence the outside service becomes known as the "token vault". The only place where there exists an association between each token and the corresponding live account number is within the token vault itself.

I won't go into the weeds of how all this works, but the end result is that the company can process credit card transactions without ever having to see the actual card numbers, a very valuable risk

---

* You know, the bad guys.

† I decided to include this small diversion as an example of how difficult it is to discuss all these topics without falling into the trap of assuming some technology background on the part of the reader. Seeing as my goal is to otherwise make the book as accessible as possible, I beg your forgiveness if anywhere in this book, I had fallen into the trap anyway.

reduction strategy, and one that comes strongly recommended in the world of credit cards due to the Payment Card Industry Data Security Standard (PCI DSS) and increasingly, is also picking up steam elsewhere.

But there are still instances when, for the purposes of some legitimate business function, the company must interact with the actual, live account number. One common instance is in loss prevention, when fraudulent transactions are investigated by an internal fraud unit, sometimes in response to law enforcement.

In a proper, secure token vault implementation, the process for reversing a token back into the original account number is done in a "side channel", that is, not on the same system that sends credit cards to the vault to obtain tokens (the "tokenizer"). The reason is simple; if all the tokenizer can do is access the vault in the one direction of converting cards to tokens, then the risk that comes from a compromise of that tokenizer is limited to whatever account numbers could be "caught" by an attacker when they are initially sent to the vault to be tokenized, and only fleetingly while they are temporarily in computer memory; those numbers are never stored locally in that system or any others attached to it.

So the tokenizer system can only convert cards to tokens. For, say, a loss prevention unit to convert a token back to a card, they might use a secure website (and a completely different authentication system) provided by the token vault provider to enter a token, which then produces back the associated card number for purposes of the investigation; doing this is called "detokenizing", and using a different path (the website) means they would be "separating the channels" of interaction with the token vault between the two processes of tokenizing and detokenizing.

But all too often, we see in the field a "single-channel" implementation. What this means is that the tokenizer is configured to be able to perform both types of activities – tokenizing and detokenizing – making it the one single channel for all card-related activities. The reason is normally that since that system already handles credit cards, then it seems like there is no additional risk involved in letting it perform both functions.

In fact, here is a dirty little secret: security people often review and authorize this approach!

Which means that no one can fault you for not immediately seeing the problem.

If the tokenizer can detokenize card numbers, then there is no actual logical separation between it and the vault itself. Once an attacker gets to the tokenizer system, they can simply execute the command to retrieve all the card numbers from the vault, which essentially serves as a database with clear text, live credit card numbers at that point. The fact that the database is (typically) hosted by someone else simply makes it a more expensive database.

It otherwise provides very little security benefit.

Which, incidentally, is exactly the same fundamental problem with storage encryption! If you have access to the system that interacts with encrypted data, then *you do not need the encryption keys to decrypt the data*. All you need is to run the process or command that retrieves the data from the encrypted data store, in full confidence that the system will successfully deal with the encryption bits, since in doing so it would be fulfilling its actual, proper, routine function.

In fact, in the cloud context, the normal form of storage encryption is almost meaningless from a security perspective – its main practical benefit is to ensure that if someone broke into, say, the AWS data center and stole the physical hard drives, they would not be able to access the underlying data easily. And considering the level of physical security in these data centers, that is a fairly remote likelihood. When you think about it, in that sense, AWS (and all other cloud infrastructure companies) are basically protecting themselves in this respect, while charging their customers for the privilege.

Yet cloud storage encryption has become a weird silver bullet that everyone chases. If you check the encryption box in AWS for that S3 bucket, you will have fulfilled your duty to most regulations that include a data security component – even if you do nothing else. That is even if the application that interacts with that bucket is full of holes, and ultimately all that encrypted data gets stolen anyway by somebody running that application to retrieve the data with the application's normal function, using a stolen non-admin user or even service credential.* Still, as a supposed data protection silver bullet, storage

---

* Again, without having ever interacted with the encryption mechanisms, or even being aware that they are in place!

encryption is captured in even more regulations passed by law makers who have little technology understanding and so take advice from people who should know better, but apparently do not choose to exercise that knowledge.

After all, isn't this the topic for this chapter?

So these guys had their tokenizer configured single channel, and now, of course, they realized that they had to protect it somehow. Which is when the truly mind-numbing design choices they had made elsewhere came to the forefront. It qualifies as a brilliant example of legacy architecture biting you in the proverbial security hiney.

See, they had built the system initially without security input, and it was "built for speed", which means they decided to neglect any authentication mechanisms. All these handshakes* would slow things down, after all. Instead, they elected to use what they euphemistically called "network-based authentication".

And what is that, you inquire? Did they do something clever in the switching layer? Was it something to do with certificates?†

Ahem.

What they meant by that was this: all of these internal systems in the network that had the tokenizer on them made the assumption that if they received any request from any other system on this network, it was to be fully trusted. They had this notion of a "network proxy" which sounded nice and provided all sorts of opportunities to argue fine technical points with any doubters, but in the end it all came down to the following principle:

Once you're in, you're in.

And when I say "in", I mean on that network segment. If you found a way into it or otherwise a system that could engage that proxy at the edge, you could issue any requests to any systems on that network without requiring any authentication whatsoever, at the system level, or user level, or any level.

Including the tokenizer.

---

* A "handshake" in authentication is the term used to refer to the process of establishing computing trust between two independent computer systems.

† Uhhh … never mind. If you get it, great, if not, it really doesn't matter, just take it as an inside joke.

I suppose I better mention that there were at least a couple of systems on the same network that provided web-based services to departments such as customer service, that were never tested for security because they were "internal only", and that the network suffered from all known common maladies, such as lack of patching. And I won't even mention the persistent access to that network – by developers.

Remember the single channel problem? Basically anyone who could find their way into any part of that environment could then utilize this assumed trust capability to kindly request the tokenizer system to retrieve all the live credit card numbers from the vault, without any authentication, and everyone would be none the wiser, on account that it was all part of the design.

The first time any form of pentest* was run against this environment, several years after it was built, the tester did exactly that, and provided a master file of the entire contents of the token vault to the company.

It took him less than 48 hours.

Of course, that freaked everybody out, as you would expect. So what did they do? Create the most convoluted "perimeter security" around that "hot zone" network, a miserable setup that involved adding two more independent layers of two-factor authentication in order to get in to the network.

Did you notice what they did not do?

They did not try to solve the underlying problem of relying on the network proxy instead of proper authentication. They effectively doubled down on the idea of trusting whoever went past the initial barrier. They made the hard taco[†] even crunchier. As anyone with any decent level of understanding of security design will tell you, that is destined to fail.

---

* A penetration test (pentest) is when you hire an ethical hacker to try and break into your systems, following the principle of "better find the holes ourselves before the bad guys do".

† This refers to the – fundamentally flawed – security idea of relying on the security perimeter, otherwise known as having a "crunchy shell and soft core", that is, as long as you make it hard to get into your environment, whatever is on the inside can stay yummy and fresh and, I suppose, not spoil. Next time you bite into that crunchy, yummy taco shell, and the back end spills its contents on your suit, you will remember this analogy and, hopefully, smile.

And it did.

Repeatedly.

It almost became an annual joke, that no matter how much they tightened those perimeter screws, the penetration tester would make a beeline for that tokenizer system and produce a list of live credit card numbers within a couple of days.

Eventually, we became involved in a big digital transformation project and were able to help drive some radical changes in the design, including the elimination of this proxy oddity and replacing it with a proper control. I still remember vividly when I was speaking to the person newly in charge of user authentication a little while afterwards, as he was asking me if there was any way we could simplify the frankly insane process of going through three different sets of different profile and two-factor systems. When I let him know that as far as I was concerned, they could now revert to a single multi-factor authentication scheme as per how people normally do things, it took him several minutes to actually believe me.

Such is the power of momentum and legacy. The longer it stays intact, the harder it is to displace. It is another, very human, trait; we come to believe that what is will always be, indeed, cannot be any different.

It feels comfortable.

Even when it is plainly wrong, and even damaging.

***

I eventually had the fortune of being able to influence some other changes and they ultimately got out from under that bonkers password scheme, too. And this issue of legacy designs leading to bad security also provides me with a perfect segue into the next chapter.

6

RUMBLE!

By now, we have discussed stories from the operational, human, legal, and technology angles of Security. But seeing as Infosec is a cross-functional discipline, related stories can often end up belonging in several of these categories all at once.

Here is another one, along this vein.

The company in question was a truly massive multinational – by far one of the largest online transactional systems in the world. It also ran a bifurcated platform, due to prior mergers and acquisitions activities that brought together a disparate set of technologies that could not be easily consolidated.

One of those platforms was originally developed on VAX machines.*

Without getting into the weeds of explaining how that came to be – the original developers did that for performance reasons – by the time that I was involved with this organization, the original hardware was long gone, but the platform still happily ran on emulators, which is software that is designed to allow running code from a different kind of machine in a virtualized environment. One way someone might encounter an emulator in common use today is by running one on their home computer to, say, play old Atari or Nintendo console games.

This system ran every transaction on the back end. It was so mission-critical that even a minute of downtime was unacceptable, let alone what they perceived to be the inevitable disruption from any attempt to migrate off of Virtual Memory System (VMS†) and into something new. On top of that, an internal culture had developed around the system, in the sense that it became the default assumption

---

* The acronym, if you care, stands for Virtual Address eXtention, and represents a very successful line of computers from the earlier digital computing era made by Digital Equipment Corporation (DEC), a former big competitor of IBM.
† Basically the VAX operating system.

DOI: 10.1201/9781003133308-7

that it could not be replaced by anything else that could perform as well as it did. No modern database would suffice, and certainly not any other kind of transactional platform. That the entire environment ran on a convoluted set of increasingly complex mechanisms to support the emulation did not deter anyone from this line of thought. Too many engineers were invested in it, for one thing, and the culture was so pervasive, that this became true of company leadership as well.

No particular harm, right? Sure. You wanna run your stuff this way, by all means, be your own guest.

But then came the credit card industry associations and that pesky payment card industry (PCI) standard.

And with it came increasingly pesky requirements to do things like monitor transactions and system events, encrypt credit card numbers in storage and in transit, and other simple controls of which, alas, VAX/VMS had no awareness. Nor could such awareness be easily developed, at least not without even more complexity that was internally determined will push the system too far, stretching it to the (performance) breaking point.

There were plenty of fascinating discussions that took place internally as the company's security people, who had fully bought into the "one true path" idea, tried to come up with compensating controls for this mess. I will share with you this one amusing tidbit, which is the reason I brought up this story in the first place: for a while, the company decided it would simply be cheaper to pay penalties ($50,000 per quarter, at least for a while) for lack of PCI compliance to a certain credit card association than to actually try and migrate into a somewhat more modern architecture.

It made sense, too. $200,000 per year is a small price to pay, and was certainly cheaper than hiring all the expertise necessary to successfully complete a migration off that infrastructure. If you will, it was simply the cost of doing business. Logical as it was from the business perspective, if you take a larger view, you could potentially come away feeling it might seem a little wrong that the company simply chose to pay penalties to a private trade association amounting to a nice full-time position (or five or six minimum wage jobs) just so as to avoid upgrading their technology stack – an upgrade that was mandated in somewhat arbitrary fashion but with the (at least superficially) noble purpose of making consumers private financial information a bit safer.

In that respect, that whole "if it ain't broke, don't fix it" mantra can lead to arguably somewhat philosophically absurd – and financially cynical – results.

***

The phone rings.

"Hey Barak", says one of my long time colleagues and friends, who runs his own consulting practice that specializes in information security.

"We have a bit of a weird problem with one of our customers, and I was wondering if maybe you had some ideas for me?"

Now, my friends, if you have stuck with me so far in this book, you know that these are the best conversations, at least when it comes to the potential generation of future stories for books that I might end up writing.

This call was, of course, no exception.

"What's up?" I ask, my funny bone starting to hum that little tune.

"So you know, we're working with these guys", he says, and then names them. Big company. Big big company. Retailer. Household name. "And we're helping them with their PCI project", he adds.

The hum gets louder, at least in my head. This fellow knows his stuff. If he is calling me to ask me about it, then it is guaranteed to be a real stumper.

"Anyway, you know how PCI needs all credit card numbers to be encrypted?" he asks, rhetorically, but I answer anyway, if only to distract myself from that incessant hum.

Put another way, I am trying really hard not to *laugh in anticipation*.

"Yeah … that little thing, sure. So …?" I add, dangling that big ol' question mark in the air.

"Well," he says, in a tone of incredulity, "see, they have these custom point of sale systems …" and he takes a pause for dramatic effect.

Oooohhhh. It's getting fun. Point of sale (POS) systems are "one of those things": they are essential, critical piping for consumer-facing businesses with a physical presence, yet they rarely get upgraded.

"And they want us to help them figure out how to encrypt the card numbers on them …" he pauses again.

Mind you, this conversation was taking place circa 2010.

Yes, this fact is important. *Quite.*

"Right?" I say. "So how can I help you?"

"Well", he says again. "These systems haven't been upgraded in a while ... they are a little, you know ... old".

"How old?" I ask. "Windows 2000 old?"

"Older", he says.

"Windows 95?" I muse.

"Yeah ... no.* Older", he responds, and I can hear the chuckle developing in his voice.

"Windows 3.11?!!!" I blurt out, incredulously.

"Close, but no cigar", he says, before dropping the hammer. "They are using a system running on DOS 5".†

A second passes in silence.

Then we both burst out laughing.

"So ..." he says, after catching his breath, "know how to encrypt card numbers on THAT?!"

I must confess that I did not.

***

These kinds of oddities happen all the time, especially as technology ages much faster than businesses do. It is one huge reason why Infosec is always struggling with attaining the ear of business leaders, at least when it is cast internally as being a technology role: there is simply no way to match speeds, if you will, between the oil tanker that is a profit and loss operation (especially a large one), and that of the evolution of the technology ocean in which it moves.‡

Remember paper records? Those things also sometimes seem to have their own inertia, like that oil tanker.

In one example, we were working with this company who provided educational courses to, umm, *people with money*.§ And because of the way, and more importantly when, they were set up, many of their

---

* In case you didn't know, "yeah no" means no and "no yeah" means yes... at least if you're speaking, uhh, *Californian*.
† Before graphical user interfaces (and Windows) existed, operating systems were running solely through the command line. This was a big one. Mind you, we're talking the Eighties here.
‡ Too complicated of an analogy? I hereby submit this as an excellent example of why I will likely never coin some "rule" that everyone will forever remember. Pity me, dear reader.
§ ... but not too much money. People with THAT kind of money have other people who manage their money for them. I mean the hopefuls and up-and-comers.

customers used a paper form to write down their credit card details to pay for their courses. Yes, my friends, this writing of card numbers on paper forms used to be a fairly common thing.

They still make you do that in some legacy hotel chains in order to reserve rooms for somebody else.

Those forms ultimately had to be kept somewhere, for regulatory reasons. In this case, they kept them in a locked file cabinet on the second floor of their nondescript office building in a similarly nondescript business park, with a security camera pointed right at that corner to make sure that they record any funny business.

Except the cabinet was always left unlocked, and the camera wasn't recording.

How do I know?

Because after pointing out that this may be an easy way for someone to steal the credit card information of reasonably high net worth individuals, especially those deliciously lovely revolving platinum American Express cards that have a high credit limit, and being pooh-poohed that there was no way it could happen and someone would catch it, I walked in one morning by purposefully tailgating someone (instead of using my assigned keycard). Then, right before lunch time, I walked in casually to the cabinet, opened it, grabbed a banker's box full of these forms, and walked out of the building together with everybody else seeking their midday nourishment. When I brought it back in to the folks in charge of security, and explained how easy it was, they immediately wanted to check the camera's recorded video feed, stating that they would be able to at least identify me as the culprit … which is when they were finally forced to admit that the camera system apparently wasn't all that, for lack of proper maintenance.

I bring this experience up because the reality is that this sort of problem is not very unusual – yet it serves to illustrate the intersection between information security (the files with the card numbers, the Internet-based security cameras and associated storage systems) and physical security (the rest). There is a reason why modern heist movies almost always involve a combination of the two.

It is an incredibly common fault line.

And were I so inclined, the amount of fraud I could likely execute successfully with the information in those forms could have been rather significant.

***

In another case involving another financial services firm, in this case a small, hybrid discount brokerage and investment house, we were performing the inaugural annual security risk assessment.

Nobody had thought to run one before we started working with them; the risk assessments they did run were all focused on the regulatory side of the house, which makes sense for this kind of business. In fact, when we were still in the initial discovery phase, we repeatedly were told that they had a strong risk management practice, and that they ran risk assessments regularly.

They had to.

It is just that the contexts of the question we asked and the answer we were given were different. That is not that unusual, actually. Let's take a little detour: I will never forget the moment when I embarrassed myself repeatedly at a senior leadership meeting at a SaaS Fintech (Software as a Service Finance Technology*) company where I had been working for only a few weeks. Because of the space in which it was operating, our sponsoring executive was the Chief Risk Officer – CRO – which is a common position in banking, and oversees regulatory compliance.†

Anyhow, at the meeting they were discussing their go-to market approach and because of the SaaS solution they were offering, it involved a particular kind of onboarding testing to emulate a scenario in which their business customers' end users‡ would have their "spending" behaviors (as in transactions) analyzed inside of the software interface.

The term being used in the meeting was "spend testing".

Spend testing.

Say it out loud and you might begin to see the proverbial egg hitting my schnozzle.

Did you get it?

No?

Well, in Security we have the concept of "pen testing", which is how we test the security of our technology systems – that whole idea

---

* Say it thrice fast while dancing all around … and an ancient curse will manifest.
† As opposed to things like SOC2 audits.
‡ It was a b2b2c play – that is, business to business to consumer. Because acronyms.

of hiring professional hackers to break into your systems so you can fix them before malicious parties can do the same.

It is just that "pen testing" and "spend testing" can sound awfully alike, especially when everything is on a video call.

You can imagine the disconnect when I took a moment to reassure the participants, all of them senior corporate leaders, by explaining how our customers would probably not need to examine our pentesting results, but even if they do, we would have the proper collateral for them. Nobody could understand what I was talking about.

For my part, I could not understand why they couldn't understand, so I tried to explain in even greater detail. I'm usually pretty good at explaining things. After all.

It was definitely not one of my best moments.

And to make it worse, this happened recently, as in, within the last couple of years. Coming off like a total idiot is a lot easier when you are not so very well known (and paid so well) for supposedly being an expert, I'll say that much.

Anyhoo ... back to the brokerage investment house guys.

So eventually we figure out the difference between "their" big-C* regulatory risk assessment and "our" small-c risk assessment, and add it to our ever-growing list of routine Infosec operational tasks to handle as part of our program management.

The time for the risk assessment arrives, and we launch the process. We know a lot about how things are set up already by then, but one thing that has been a bit of a mystery has been how they were running their IT department; the core business functions, running on servers in a data center, were managed by an "investment technology operations" guy, but the back-office functions and laptop management seemed a little less ... organized.

For one thing, nobody ever asked us anything about IT since we started working with them. While we usually use our own laptops in our engagements, there is often at least some interaction with IT to ensure that we won't be endangering their environment, and for them to assign us internal emails, that sort of thing.

Nothing of the sort here.

Also, everybody seemed to use different laptop brands.

---

* The "C" (or "c") here stands for compliance.

It seemed important to gain a better insight into those practices.

I will never forget the moment when we finally got the answers we were looking for. We were sitting in this second-floor conference room, which was directly and easily accessible from the outside, on the inside of a hybrid mall/office building. They had wall to wall TV screens mounted around the entire room, a huge whiteboard, and a standing closet of sorts.

The lady we were chatting with was an executive assistant to the leadership group. She was also, we came to learn, a sort of makeshift IT person. She did not have a lot of understanding of IT, but she knew how to order stuff if anyone needed it. One thing they apparently ordered a lot of were external hard drives; she showed us a pile of them in the closet.

And why did they need those, you wonder?

Ah.

Glad you asked.

The reason they did not really need anyone managing things like laptops is that the company simply didn't have any.

I do not mean to say that nobody used laptops. In fact, most of them (everyone except the traders on the floor) did.

It is just that the company did not feel like it needed to own or supply them to employees. Instead, everyone was essentially expected to use their own. The brokers had their company-owned trading terminals, of course, but that was that. They started out when desktops were the big thing, and as the technology landscape shifted into laptops, they never built (or, seemingly, cared to build) the necessary processes to handle that shift – even as the employees themselves adopted a laptop as their primary (in fact, only) computer. Desktops were retired and never replaced. The company did reimburse some of the people for buying those laptops, yes, but did not consider them company property nor managed the devices in any way.

And those external drives? They were how employees were expected to store company data while using their own laptops, and they would return them when they were done with them, say at termination of employment.

You can have a field day with all of these assumptions.

One additional interesting side effect was their backup and recovery strategy. Because of those external hard drives, they felt that they could always recover from any disaster, because all the data was "distributed" across multiple "backup sites" – that is, at the homes of employees. In fact, they carried this approach further, and actually sent (non-encrypted, of course – why do you ask?) hard drives with trading data home with certain employees for safe keeping. Some of those drives also ultimately ended up in that closet. You could easily take them and all that precious financial data on them with you, if you were so inclined.

Apparently, they even managed to use this strategy successfully to satisfy their regulatory compliance requirements, too. Which again shows, incidentally, the enormous chasm between compliance and the mechanics of security.

***

That bit about using employees' homes as a method for "distributed backup" is actually much less crazy than it appears, and even has an incredibly common modern parallel, right here and now in 2021.

Just go talk to a vice president (VP) of engineering or Chief Technical Officer (CTO) of any number of cloud SaaS/Platform as a Service (PaaS) companies out there. Ask them how they back up their software code, which for most of them is managed in a cloud repository (AKA repo) called Github.

What happens when Github fails? Maybe you lose the repo because someone fat-fingers the administrative account? Or worse, does so maliciously? Another very common aspect of many of these setups is that they use engineers' personal accounts (instead of corporate ones) to provide access to company software assets, and while this works fine for smaller teams, it can get messy as they grow.

So how do you recover if something goes kablooey?

Without question, the most common answer you will get if you ask the question is this one: "well, Github uses a distributed method of handling code, so developers all have portions of the code tree stored locally on their laptops. If we absolutely have to, we can reconstruct all our code from the laptops".

That statement is factual and fundamentally correct. Indeed, developer laptops will likely, in the aggregate, contain all the code that the company manages in Github, and you could, in theory, reassemble it as necessary if something bad happens.

Here's the thing though, the proverbial "devil is in the details" follow-up question:

Have you actually tried doing it?

Because it is not that simple if you have many engineers with different levels of access to different code repos, and if you have to do it while the survival of your business is on the line ... let me just suggest that there are probably more enjoyable ways to pass one's time.

Like getting a quadruple root canal.

While your knee undergoes an arthroscopy.

In other words, it would probably not be the smoothest, most pleasant experience.

Yet many, many companies are run with the assumption that this is not only possible, but easy to accomplish. In a rather big way, it is testament to just how good is cloud Github; if that sucker suffers a catastrophic failure, the knock-on effects will be brutal, as a mind-boggling number of cloud companies go dark for an undetermined amount of time, "assembling their code base from the laptops".

Or, to use professional lingo ... it will be fun times.

**

Occasionally, it is the nature of the organization itself that can lead to dramatic, and unusual, information security moments. While most of my own experience has been in the for-profit world, it certainly is not limited to commercial operations.

And once you cross the threshold into, say, big government, suddenly things can take on a completely different character. For one thing, the person in charge of security can have real teeth to enforce their authority, something that is often not the case in the private sector.

Back in the days when the Federal Information Security Management Act (FISMA) security standard was being developed following the passage of the relevant regulation, I was spending some time working independently as a sub at a large government installation. It was very early days in operating my new consulting venture, the one that eventually became EAmmune. My role was fairly limited, in assessing and documenting relevant controls pertaining to FISMA compliance, but I still enjoyed my time there as it was quite a different experience from working at various private companies.

They ran their own big onsite data center, and had a Chief Information Officer (CIO) who was also put in charge of information security, and consequently, owned the whole FISMA compliance program. She was very much a no-nonsense kind of executive, expected that IT and engineering staff would follow through on their commitments and deadlines, and was more than happy to use all the tools at her disposal to ensure that they would, in fact, do so.

I was working on a section of the control matrix which had particularly egregious control failures, and as I became friendly with the permanent staff, I learned that there was some internal power struggle between the folks responsible for this area and the CIO. Essentially, and without putting too fine a point on it, the former thought that the FISMA requirements were idiotic and dragged their feet about implementing them, whilst the latter knew that as the person in charge, it was her head that would roll if they could not get out from under an "F" (as in Fail) ranking with respect to said controls.

It was also my personal impression, which could therefore be entirely wrong, that those engineers resented having to report to a woman CIO.

They simply did not respect her.

This went back and forth for a while, and I got a decent view of it because I was the person documenting the progress of, or lack thereof, implementing the relevant controls. Definitely not what you might call front row seats, but not in the nosebleeds either. The fellow who brought me in as a sub – let's call him Steve – was in direct communications with the CIO, and gave me a lot of insights with respect to said inside baseball.

In and of itself, it was a great education.

Anyway, fast forward a few months. The heat is increasing constantly in this battle of wills, and on my end I get a little uncomfortable because I constantly have to report that no progress is being made on control implementation. One day I arrive at the facility, go through the security checks, and get to the office where I had been working.

Things already look weird as I walk the hallways, with people shuffling idly about in what was definitely an unusual fashion.

I get to the office.

Steve is sitting there in his chair, musing. Normally he would be typing furiously at this hour, but instead, his computer is idle and he is just reading some manual.

"Hey Steve", I say, as I start setting myself up.

"Don't bother", he says, and I stop. Am I being fired?

"All the systems are down", he adds. As he sees the question mark in my eyes, he says "yeah, can't tell you much more yet, but they ain't coming back on today".

Then, as I close the lid to my laptop slowly (maybe even forlornly), he adds, "no, stick around, it's not you. You're still getting paid. I promise I'll fill you in later".

Later turned out to be the afternoon, and that was when I learned how authority works when it actually means something, like, say, in a big government facility.

See, the CIO had another frustrating meeting with engineering leadership, where she again met the same resistance to getting the things she wanted done, done. Her initial FISMA auditing deadline was coming up, and she was determined not to get failing marks.

Apparently, the exchange got pretty heated.

The way Steve told it to me, she gave them an ultimatum: fix it or else. And they decided to call her on it and issued their own, reverse challenge. The thing with ultimatums is that they are a high-risk play … and if you calculate wrong, they can blow up in your face … in either direction.

Like it did here.

So the CIO got out of her chair, and walked down to the data center. I can imagine her footsteps echoing in the hallway as the senior engineers were following behind her sullenly. And when she got to the data center …

She shut off the (user) network.

Quite literally, turned it all down by removing power from a critical network switch.

Then she turned to those engineering leaders, who were staring at her in disbelief, and told them, simply, that unless and until they implemented the control in question, that switch would not be powered back on.

And she carried her threat through. Amazingly, it took only three days for the issue to be resolved to her satisfaction. But they were some of the most interesting "non-working" working days I had ever experienced, as the resisters realized that they were, in point of fact, both in the wrong and outgunned in the matter.

They were going through the five stages of grief right in front of my eyes.

***

Cross-disciplinary situations like this one can get particularly fraught – or satisfying, depending on your point of view and role as either, ah, victim or problem solver – when it comes to the intersection of regulatory compliance and IT security.

This is overwhelmingly due to one simple reason: laws and regulations are written slowly, and technology in our current technology age advances extremely rapidly. When one tries to capture any sort of prescriptive technology guidance in a regulation, the end result is inevitably guaranteed to lead to perverse outcomes. And all of that gets even more complicated as lawmakers generally are not technology savvy; they do have another job, after all, which is politics.

Then it goes from the sausage-making to the field, and corporate lawyers get their hands on it. Their specialty, of course, is to protect their clients from liability, so that is the only lens through which they view the regulation, which often serves to distort the intent and purpose of the already badly drafted rule, and it is all downhill from there.

You can see this every time some new regulation attempts to tackle data security and privacy. For example, the Gramm-Leach-Bliley Act (GLBA), passed in 1999, has a section around data protection for consumers financial information. Thankfully GLBA is not particularly prescriptive, but let's be honest: do you even remember what our world looked like in the late Nineties, from a technology perspective? Yet the GLBA security rule can be the primary driver of security control design and implementation in many a financial institution. In the modern context, it can be … somewhat lacking.

Oh, I know, GLBA is not prescriptive, and the security rule gets revised from time to time, and this and that. I hear this all the time. Here is what I also know: banks, even the largest ones, generally have terrible security postures in many parts of their technology environment. They protect their interests (so their "money systems" have good controls), and everything else often ends up in the "do we need it for GLBA?" bucket, to which the answer is usually "nah, we're fine without it".

Like ... non-encrypted networked ATM systems, running on obsolete Windows operating systems, sitting on the same end user network as the employees, meaning that any internal user can get to any ATMs backend without even going through an internal firewall?

Sure, I've seen it.

Why not?

"If somebody tries something we'll catch it on the server".

That kind of stuff is a dime a dozen.

Still, there are much worse offenders. Here is one: the Healthcare Insurance Portability and Accountability Act (HIPAA), also from the Nineties, has a security rule of its own. In it, it defines something called Patient Health Information (PHI), and also its electronic version (ePHI). It then counts eighteen different categories of Personally Identifiable Information (PII), which, when they exist in conjunction with someone's health condition or care (or payment for such care), together become PHI.

Many of these PII categories are very familiar to anyone who has had to interact with privacy rules: names, phone numbers, addresses, and IP addresses. Some are more specific to the industry, such as health insurance ID numbers. But they are still just PII, according to HIPAA.

All this makes sense so far? Good, because here is how it breaks down in our modern world super quick, now to the point of being fundamentally, institutionally broken.

Keep in mind that HIPAA was drafted a long time ago, when some hidden assumptions were sort of baked into the thinking. One such assumption, that HIPAA also shares with GLBA and other rules from the era, was that companies owned their information systems. In today's world of 2021, this assumption is, of course, laughable; that is, everybody's moving to the cloud, abstraction layers abound, and nobody owns anything fully anymore.

Where this creates a persistent failure is in the way covered healthcare entities – those subject to HIPAA – over-interpret the rule, or at least how their lawyers do so. To bring this into focus, we need a bit more context, so bear with me. HIPAA recognizes that the enforcement role of the regulator – Health and Human Services (HHS) – is limited to only those organizations which it regulates. It similarly recognizes that these organizations will have to rely on unregulated third parties to perform many business functions, which in some cases would involve the sharing of PHI. How can HHS ensure that PHI remains protected once it leaves the regulated domain?

This is a problem that is shared with privacy rules, and is typically solved in a similar way. In HIPAA's case, the regulation sets up the idea of a Business Associate Agreement (BAA), wherein the regulated ("covered") entity compels its third parties that are involved in managing its core regulated processes – that is, provisioning and paying for healthcare – to maintain a minimum level of information security for PHI. So, for example, say a hospital engages a third-party medical billing provider to handle payments; the hospital will then execute a BAA with the billing provider, which should hopefully serve to ensure that protection of PHI is more or less consistent even as it is being exchanged between the two. HIPAA even defines what types of third parties would require a BAA, and they are generally what you would expect: the kinds of organizations involved in healthcare provisioning and payment facilitation.

Alright, this should be good enough for our purposes,* that is: to comply with HIPAA, regulated entities must use BAAs whenever they share PHI with certain third parties, with the accompanying hidden underlying (and increasingly faulty) assumption that companies generally own their information systems.

Here is what happens in real life today.

In real life, the lawyers for many of those covered entities have by and large adopted the conservative posture that any service provider they use in the IT space must also sign a BAA. This emerging trend has become a sort of de-facto modus operandi, especially when it comes to cloud-based software and platforms, because they keep proliferating rapidly with new, sexy solutions that enterprises want to

---

* If you are reading this and you are actually in the industry, you probably have many objections to my hand wavey approach in explaining this, but keep in mind, this is a stories book, not a HIPAA book.

make use of, and also present all these weird challenges in terms of who owns what, where.

And I do mean, everyone. Payroll SaaS company? BAA. Cloud-based malware protection? BAA. Online document store for human resources? BAA. BAA, BAA. Many young SaaS vendors end up taking the approach that they might as well sign these things, because the lawyers on the other side insist and the SaaS vendor knows it's not dealing with PHI anyway, so where's the harm? The more conscientious ones try to argue their position, but are quickly overwhelmed by the need to close the deal.

Of course, there is harm: signing these kinds of agreements creates all sorts of hidden liabilities and potential future headaches. This kind of practice may also dilute the value of the commercial protections otherwise put in place.

Even putting all that aside, the truly astonishing aspect of it all is this: there is nothing in HIPAA that actually drives any of this.

See, the part everyone seems to forget (or willfully ignore) is that PHI only comes into being when an individual's PII is combined with their healthcare information.* Say you are a hospital and you share your patients' names and emails with a SaaS company that runs marketing surveys on your behalf. Listen, folks: even though you are a covered entity, and this PII belongs to your patients, *this does not make it PHI!* it sure is still PII, and subject to privacy rules, but do leave the BAA alone for this one.

It is not actually needed or necessary.

Oh, I can imagine a bunch of you jumping up and down right now in excitement, relishing the moment of proving me wrong (and knowing that I cannot fix it, either; once a book is out, it is out forever). Well, this is where I go back to this collective groupthink decision by the corporate lawyers of covered entities who had done this legal analysis and determined that yes, in fact, this would constitute PHI because it indicates a medical relationship between that patient and that hospital, which the survey company now apparently "knows" about, thereby making them a business associate.

Baloney, dear reader.

Baloney.

---

* As a reminder, this means condition, care, or payments.

Without getting this into heated argument territory, I will just add this: a colleague of mine, let's call him Jim, was actually a advising lawyer to the committee that drafted this rule. You cannot get much closer to real intent, in other words. So one day, as I grew increasingly frustrated with this repeated inanity, I reached out to Jim and asked him about it. I described several of these scenarios. In particular, I talked about scenarios where the covered entity in question shared classic PII, say, their patients' email addresses and names in a context that was unrelated to provisioning health services. In one example, I described measuring the performance of a healthcare company's mobile app – in other words, a common analytics use case that companies of all stripes rely upon all the time. Sure, consumers interact with the app for healthcare purposes, but these third party measurements engage at a lower level, to evaluate things like ease of use of the app. These analyses are entirely unaware and devoid of the healthcare data layer.

Anyways, we chat about this and that for a while, and then I ask him the million dollar question: "Jim, does the fact that the mobile app is published by a covered entity means that this PII suddenly, automatically becomes PHI? Does it mean that now the PaaS company is a business associate by receiving it, even though the data involved really has nothing to do with the provisioning of healthcare?"

After rolling his eyes, his response was as clear cut as you would ever get from any lawyer, and delivered in the appropriately dry fashion:

"When the rule was drafted, we never intended for PII by itself to be considered PHI".

Then he added, even more dryly, "there are privacy laws for that".

And that, my friends, is that.

7
BACK TO BASICS

Back when this whole madness of working for myself began, I was really mostly just trying to survive. I certainly did not envision that any idea that I might have, especially one that felt easily discardable like serving in the capacity of fractional, "virtual Chief Information Security Officer (vCISO)", would take hold as well as it has. Sufficiently so, in fact, that I would not only still be doing it some 20 years later, but that it would result in a thriving consulting and services firm delivering security program management to so many companies. That this concept has become a common method for many different types of organizations to engage with the rapidly emerging discipline of Information Security, to such a degree that demand for it far exceeds the supply of available, experienced talent, and that my own firm has grown as much as it already has, continues to leave me with a sense of wonder.

That I am, as I type this, writing the last chapter of my *second* book revolving around this topic would have seemed downright fantastical.

Still, I am nothing if not practical, and my view of Information Security as anchored in psychology and behaviors more than technology systems has in itself led to some amusing stories along the way.

For example, back when I was in survival mode, I became convinced by this idea that as a security leader, it is essential that I understand the field of Sales. Not just superficially, but fundamentally – that is, how it really works. It is a little bit of that hacker mentality, I suppose, but through a people lens.

This view was built on my extremely fortunate exposure to the world of business development in the context of mergers and acquisitions during my last year at Netvision, in Israel – before I relocated to California.

DOI: 10.1201/9781003133308-8

At the time Netvision was such a hotbed of activity, with the Internet bubble inflating red hot and at full pitch. I had developed a strong interest in business administration, so I asked my CEO at the time – an early Internet pioneer, glass shattering, kickass lady by the name of Ruth Alon to whom I will forever be grateful for her mentorship and kindness in those extremely early stages of my career – if I could do something more along the business operations lines. I desperately wanted to learn. She made me promise to keep supporting the technology side of the company, helped me get signed up for MBA school with a lovely recommendation, and assigned me to work for the vice president of business development as an analyst. That was one of the best years of my professional life, giving me an inside look into so much of the inner workings of capital investment, management, and cash flows, and all those invisible pipes in the walls that make them all come together, and I got to learn all of that in one of the hottest companies in the country in the hottest moment at the hottest sector.

You really can't pay for this kind of education. You just have to be lucky enough to be there when it happens.

I had previously struck up a strong friendship with the enterprise sales team, learning how essential it was to project a mature technology posture to large customers, and just as importantly, how to do so effectively. In other words, I was already inclined to pursue this direction of being a … what would be the right term? Sales nerd? "Sales engineers" did not yet exist at the time, but in retrospect, I certainly filled that role while also doing the network architecture and Internet routing stuff.

I cherished every moment of it.

As a side note, if you're interested in pursuing a security management career in a for-profit technology business, I would suggest that spending some time doing sales engineering would be a terrific way to learn what actually matters and develop that "gut sense" for business risk so crucial to the discipline.

Fast forward a few years, and I am struggling to build an individual consulting practice, and to simply survive. America may be the land of opportunity, but it sure is not very good at giving people the basic safety net necessary at the bottom end of the scale so they could harness whatever creativity and drive they might have to make it all come together.

One thing that I was not doing very well was selling. Surely, I got a customer here and there, but I had left a mid-six-figure corporate job, and it took years to get back there on my own. Let me tell you, it is an experience that can be pretty deflating.

So one summer morning I found myself in front of the mirror. I was determined to break through the awkwardness. I had to learn this system. I had to crack it so that I could make it work for me. And for the next couple of weeks, I did it every morning, for as long as I could suffer through it, which really wasn't very long on most days.

I sold me to myself.

***

Such efforts had resulted in some amusing side effects. A rather noticeable one is evident simply because it is difficult for many people to accept that a CISO can be both super nerdy while at the same time sporting a human-friendly user interface (UI). In fact, while it really helps with doing the job well, it can also sometimes breed resentment and suspicion from within the ranks. Put another way, while people who are not in security generally respond well to having a security leader who is not constantly running around scaring everybody, some security people will have the exact opposite reaction, turning away in disgust, often muttering dark incantations under their breath.

Sometimes, they end up trying to prove the lack of substance and expose what they consider to be "the fraud". I ran into this phenomenon on two occasions that I am aware of, as they pertained directly to me.

In one such case, I had been chatting with a friend of mine, who has been working as a security architect for what had felt like forever in a large financial institution. But that "forever" started after I had met him, which was when he was working as a consultant.

His (real) name is Kaya.

Kaya and I first ran into each other at a customer of mine, during the time when I was still mostly operating in sole proprietor mode. I was running their security program which also involved managing the payment card industry (PCI) program for them, and he appeared out of the blue to, as I was told, help support the upcoming PCI audit process. I did not need the help, but also did not mind it, plus he was a really cool guy and was super intelligent and fun, and I love meeting new and interesting people.

He also seemed to know PCI pretty well, and he asked me all sorts of probing and detailed questions about that and the security program in general.

Then after a few months his contract with the company ended and he went on to get hired by that big financial institution.

Flash forward to this more recent conversation. We were chatting about some of our perspectives in the field and the topic switched to that first joint experience.

"Barak, I have to tell you something", he suddenly says to me.

"Yeah? What?" I was curious.

"You remember when we were working together back then, and I was helping you with the PCI project?"

"Sure", I responded, wondering where this was heading.

"Well", he said, "did you ever realize that it was not what I was actually doing?"

I was dumbfounded. Took me a second to find my voice again.

"So … what were you doing then?" I asked.

"I was auditing you", he responded with a casual tone and a glint in his eye.

"You were … what?" I was having trouble parsing the words.

"I was auditing you", he repeated. "They got me in there to make sure you weren't being a fraud, basically".

Well, that was certainly an intriguing twist.

I asked him to clarify.

Turns out that, while they really appreciated the fact that I seemed to find what felt like "magical solutions" to some big challenges the company was facing, at the same time they grew suspicious that I might be fooling everyone instead. So one of the executives called one of his friends, who owned a consulting company with expertise in information security and audits,* and asked him for some extra hands – and to double check on me, see if I was legit, or if I was putting the company at undue risk.

There really isn't a nice way to say it: they wanted to make sure I was not lying.

So that was how Kaya came to be involved with them. The funny thing was, he told me that he really tried to prove that I was screwing

---

* Who has also, incidentally, become a good friend of mine since then.

around, but couldn't; every time he tried to poke holes at what I might have been doing, the answers I gave him, he told me, were sensible, reasonable, and effective. His biggest criticism was, in fact, that I consciously chose to believe the answers provided by other people in the company to the questions I had asked them. But even then, he understood my motivation in that context; my goal was not to "discover" any omissions or even surface straight-up lies, but rather to help the company move towards its compliance goal while keeping them at arm's length from their auditor, the result of which would in turn support the company's business goals.

Eventually, Kaya admitted, he came to appreciate what I was doing and how I was doing it, and we ended up being friends instead, something that has lasted to this very day.

I still think that it ended up being a rather pleasing conclusion.

***

Being audited is, of course, part of the job description in this field, so the above is not all *that* unusual – especially not if you recall some of the horror stories I shared with you earlier in this book. Security is a trust business, which naturally also makes it a *mis*trust business. These dynamics are perhaps amusingly illustrated in the story around *Catch Me if You Can*, that delightful Hollywood caper movie that was supposedly based on the life of one Frank Abagnale Jr., conman extraordinaire. It is without question a fun flick, and one part of it that is certainly true is that Mr. Abagnale made a nice career in security for himself following his prison stint (in his case, his expertise was in check fraud, but it is still all part of the Security discipline).

Lovely as it is, why do I bring up this movie? Because if you dig deeper, it is not entirely clear that the stories about Mr. Abagnale, the ones that form the basis for the movie, are in themselves factually true. In fact, extensive investigations into his claims have all tended to conclude that most or even all of those claims are, at best, vastly exaggerated. When you think about it, this is a rather remarkable, continuing sort of con: small-time fraud until one gets caught and goes to jail, followed by a sort of marketing con to elevate the impact of the original offenses in order to build one up as a sort of criminal mastermind, ultimately using this image to develop a new career in crime fighting … which then allows one to burnish one's reputation and continue to evolve the story until one becomes the hero of a Hollywood production, forever cementing the bigger con about the smaller con as holy writ.

Kind of admirable, in its own way.

And very apt in the security field, at least if you think about it in people terms. There is a wonderful lesson to learn from this, which is that a good storyteller will pretty much always defeat any security system, simply by virtue of being able to manipulate the *operators* of said system. This is the essence of social engineering, if you have ever run across the term. Just go back to the Analyzer story I shared with you in Chapter 2, and you will see what I mean; there were actual newspaper clippings (and even one clip from a local TV station) that pronounce how I "caught" this hacker! How easy would it be to slip that into my background? Would it ever be challenged? And it certainly could be helpful to my career to restate that claim as often as possible, especially since I am not the one who ever made the claim in the first place.

But as much as I love to observe the people who are able to sustain these kinds of stories, this kind of borrowed fame has (unfortunately perhaps) never appealed to me. Heck ... to be brutally honest, it scares the hell out of me. It is also why I am always very careful to note that it is only as far as I know that I originated the "virtual CISO". All I can say with confidence is that to this point, no one has claimed otherwise. I suppose that makes sense, since as an idea, it isn't particularly clever; it is, after all, just another business services concept.

***

Speaking of being audited, I had another occasion in which I was, unbeknownst to me, examined by someone who was determined to expose me. This particular story is one I truly cherish, because of the circumstances surrounding it.

Before I tell you the story, I need to very briefly explain how my services organization, EAmmune, works; fundamentally, instead of having employees or contractors, it instead consolidates (or at least initially and for a fair while did so) a fair number of small, highly experienced, independent business to business (b2b) operators (essentially, vendors) under its service delivery umbrella. There are many excellent reasons for constructing it that way, but this is not the book to discuss them. Most importantly, it is a highly pragmatic approach to delivering services. I only ask that you accept, at least for the moment, that there is a very solid argument as to why this not only works well; it is by far the best way to organize for all the stakeholders involved. However, at the same time this sort of structure can sound a bit odd if you have never encountered something like it before.

Anyway, I was giving a talk at the San Francisco east bay Information Systems Audit and Control Association (ISACA) chamber, and it went pretty well. At one point I mentioned that EAmmune was growing, and after the session, one of the participants, Sue (real name again), approached me as we left the building to introduce herself. She said that she found the talk interesting, and also wanted to see if there might be a fit between her skills and experience and our needs. Well, I could tell fairly rapidly that there would be, so we chatted for a while.

Sue told me more about herself, and I explained in greater detail what we did and how we operated, and why EAmmune is so much of a lifestyle opportunity, and we ultimately agreed to discuss things further yet. I introduced her to our other two organizational leaders, after which she spoke to the team, and eventually joined forces with us, like everybody else who does, on a trial basis. She already had her own small individual consulting practice in place so in that sense, there was not much, if any, onboarding friction.

About six months later we were chatting about this and that and the other, and she was telling me that she was going to bring her good friend to talk with us as well, because she thought there might be a good fit there, too. She was right, and they did join us and are also now part of EAmmune, something that in itself gives me a great deal of pleasure. But that is not the reason I bring up Sue's story. The reason, or maybe the funny part, is this: see, Sue came from a deep security and financial auditing background. Her entire, impressive professional career has been spent in finding and identifying faults in the way companies went about their business. What she admitted to me next was that when she joined forces with us, it was because she was convinced that what I was telling her was some sort of scam – and she was determined to expose it.

In other words, and entirely unbeknownst to me, Sue came in to prove us wrong and tear us down. And she admitted that she looked everywhere she could, just like my friend Kaya did above, only to come up empty, and with a newly found appreciation of the somewhat off the beaten path, highly efficient and pragmatic nature of it all.

In an even more amusing footnote, Sue – a lady who would downright scare me were I to run an organization that was audited by her actually knowing something was wrong, because she is so good at digging that she would 100% find whatever it was – is now responsible for referring to us about a third of our present staff. Or the way she put it to me when I asked her permission to share this story …

Start from believing it's a scam, instead make it a cult.

Maybe we should make that into a company t-shirt.

***

One thing I do get asked a lot is "how do you do it?"

That is, being CISO is considered in itself a fairly demanding role. While my thoughts on the subject are well known, there is no question that serving in this role for, say, four companies at once, while also being CEO (and, for all intents and purposes, CFO) of your own company can occasionally be … distracting. I mean, being human, I cannot actually multitask,* but the rapid context switching throughout a typical day can sometimes get to be awfully fierce.

As a relevant (for me) side note, I do find it intriguing when I hear the claim, from some industry insiders, that because I am not a full-time employee anywhere, I apparently do not have a true reputational stake in doing a good job as a security chief. This idea is even captured into some enterprise security questionnaires ("who is your full-time CISO?"). The level of ignorance shown by this statement is breathtaking, once you consider that a boutique consulting organization like ours lives and dies by its reputation, and that my own professional reputation is tightly coupled to the success of security management and governance in each and every one of dozens of accounts. That is, my own personal and professional reputational risk, as ultimately would be reflected by making idiotic decisions, is dramatically higher than that of any full-time CISO, anywhere, because it involves many more organizations.

---

* According to science, our brains really can't do that. Or maybe it's simply because I'm a man.

It is easily higher than the risk of getting fired after a breach, which is pretty much the entirety of the risk normally faced by a CISO. More importantly, because getting fired after a breach is often an unspoken yet instinctively understood part of the role, it does not mean the end of their career – just a new employer.

Anyway.

As I mentioned, all of that context switching can get challenging.

One Monday in the mid-Tens,* I was facing a somewhat more involved version of a typical afternoon setup; starting at 1 PM, I had seven back to back 30-minute calls, each one with a different group at a different customer organization, but with me fulfilling the role of CISO for each and every one.

A normal Monday might have four or five such calls, with some space in between, so seven in a row was a tad more than usual, but what made this particular series contextually difficult to handle was this: in each one of the calls, at some point during the conversation, somebody wanted to bring up something and in order to do so, employed some variation of the following phrase:

"Well,† Jessica said …" (AKA the "essica Clause").

Yes, they all had a Jessica.

And each of the Jessicas was involved, somehow, in each of the conversations.

Do you recall the infamous Windows "blue screen of death"?‡

So this is what happened, which also happens to be one of my most memorable and amusing failures: as call number seven started, my brain was feeling a little sluggish. Then, within two minutes, the "Jessica clause" popped up in the conversation.

And my brain blue-screened to death.

I suddenly found myself utterly frozen, unable to comprehend any words being said on the call. I went into a spiral.

"With whom am I having this conversation?"

"Which company is it?"

"What is the topic we're on about?"

---

* Is that what you call the 201x decade? I wasn't sure.

† The "well" could be a "but" or an "and", but the important bit was all the Jessicas.

‡ If you are too young to remember it, just Google it. It used to be a meme before memes existed.

And then the inevitable thought exploded in my brain like a mortar shell.

"Who … the hell … *is Jessica?*"

After a few seconds of mounting terror, I took a deep breath and waited for the person on the other end to finish a question they were asking me, of which I could make zero sense. Then I replied saying that my brain had apparently suffered a fatal crash, and that I needed to reboot before we proceed.

Everyone laughed, assuming I was joking. I assured them that I was not. Then I put myself on mute, closed my eyes, breathed deeply a few times, and calmed myself down. Next I opened up my calendar, looked up the meeting invite, and used that to recover the context for that call.

Thirty seconds later I got back on, deeply embarrassed or, as a certain famous British spy would put it, shaken, not stirred.

***

One more question that I have been asked a number of times before is why I had not chosen to write a more instructional book, full of step by step "how to" guides, a kind of "Security Management for Dummies" manual.

I do not really have a great answer for that, except for a rather simple one that I venture is going to come across as mildly ignorant: I wouldn't read it myself. I have seen those books. I own some of them. They are very impressive tomes, with appropriately large spines, and shiny covers, and some of them are even in color, and you can quite literally feel the weight of them as you pick them up.

Heck, my publisher, the folks who will have printed this manuscript in book form by the time you hold it in your hands, are arguably the best experts in sourcing and compiling these kinds of books. The very series* that this book is a part of is largely like that, and so was *Why CISOs Fail*, even though neither that book nor this one have much to do at all with IT Audit.

But here is the truth, or at least my truth: when I try to read those books, I get bored so very quickly. I was a terrible student when I was still going to high school, and later college at the Technion in Israel,

---

* The "IT Audit" series, by Dan Swanson.

and earned my degree with a combination of luck, charm, and chutz-pah, as much as anything else. My mind wonders in these settings. But give me a good story, and I will get sucked into it like any ol' planet would be by coming too near to the event horizon of a massive black hole. I have read well over 2,000 books in my life, and you can bet your sweet ass the majority of them were story-based or some kind of fiction, rather than the reporting or instructional kinds.

I recall very recently when I was interviewing candidates for the position of full-time CISO at one of EAmmune's customer organiza-tions who were graduating from our program. We started working with them when they were very small, did the things we do to support their rapidly growing business, and ultimately got to the point with them when it finally made sense for them to "insource" the security department. It is likely that by the time this book hits the printers that they will have gone through their initial public offering (IPO), which, for better or worse, is often when companies that utilize our services choose to make this transition.

Interviews can be funny things. To me, the purpose of one is to get a sense of the person sitting in front of you. By this point, it likely would not come as a shock to you if I told you that I hold a rather dim view of the rather insane attempts by companies like Google to hire "perfectly". Just like any other process gone amok, all of their elaborate processes end up being in service to them-selves, and as a result the company misses out on tons of remark-ably clever, creative, and motivated candidates who fail to "fit" their exact mold. I firmly believe that you cannot "operationalize" humans this way, at least not without breeding a strong culture of uniformity and obedience. This can work just fine when you are in a strong position in a leading industry, but makes you extremely vulnerable to future disruption. Still, it clearly seems to work for Google and others who have taken to emulating them, so who am I to judge?

My own approach is rather different, as you might expect. When I interview candidates, I try to challenge their thinking and engage with their feelings – not by coming up with impossible questions and scoring them against some chart on how obscure their knowledge base might be – but rather by asking simple questions with broad applicability and tons of room for interpretation, and then observing *how* they answer while letting the ensuing conversation go where it naturally wants to go.

Will they share their thought process with me? Will they take a leap of faith, or shut down because they feel uncomfortable? Will they ask me for clarification? Will they admit to not having a good answer, or even (gasp) not knowing?* All of these are, to me, far more important than whether they know any specific detail about any particular technology or what have you. In Security Operations (SecOps), for example, it is my firmly established opinion that it is far, far easier to teach security than it is to teach self-discipline – and it is why I always suggest that this realm is particularly well suited for veterans. SecOps succeeds or fails on the strength of its members' self-discipline, not the underlying technologies upon which it relies. And the army is, after all, really, really good at teaching self-discipline, not to mention teamwork and self-reliance, both of which are hugely beneficial core principles in SecOps. Thus, in my opinion, veterans are natural candidates for SecOps.

In this vein, one of my favorite questions to pop to any candidate for a security leadership position, such as a CISO or VP of Security, is this very simple one – do you have a security management philosophy? You would be surprised by just how much people are caught off guard when they are asked this question. And yet, if you really are in this field for what I would consider real reasons – if you are passionate about it, and have spent any serious amount of time trying to master it† – then you would have by necessity developed a philosophy of some kind in how you handle it. Otherwise, the men in white coats would have inevitably come and taken you to a safe place at some point.

And so, in going back to the main narrative, in this one interview I received one of my favorite answers ever. One that I would myself be proud to give in response to this question – and have in fact in the past. I just never heard anyone else refer to it that way. The candidate, Olivia, initially registered surprise (as pretty much everyone does when I ask this question), but took it in stride. She thought about it for a couple of seconds, then looked back to me through the Zoom screen and said, simply:

---

* A cardinal sin in the world of Google and its emulators.
† ... before realizing it's impossible.

"It's an art form".

Then she started laughing, with what I thought was a bit of discomfort, probably wondering how I would take that answer.

Of course I loved it. How could I not? If you have enough experience, confidence, and human skillz to pull off this sort of succinct and simple answer then it tells me much more about your connection to the field than any whiteboard filled with smart equations ever could. It led to a delightful 20-minute conversation about how she saw it that way and why, and there was no question in my mind that she would make a terrific CISO for any company.

By the way, to this day I have never really read her resume.

I hope she forgives me when she reads this.

***

So is this it?

Have I run out of stories to share?

Of course not. It may be that the trickiest bit of writing a book like this* is in picking the stories out of a multitude of them. This task was further complicated by all the stories I had previously shared in *Why CISOs Fail*, because I wanted to avoid repeating any of those.† Also, and in a similar fashion to *Why CISOs Fail*, I decided to keep this manuscript to a similar size overall, which has driven my selection of stories to a reasonable amount. I did that for the same reason as I did last time: it is a lot less intimidating to read any book when it isn't … you know …

Massive.

And I actually wanted you to read it.

My greatest hope is that as you have gone through these pages, you might have gleaned some useful insights for yourself. That you found some of these stories relatable, even as others may have been shocking. That it has given you a sense of relief, maybe even eased the daily dread of dealing with this scary topic. After all, this stuff happens to everyone – and I'll be first in line to admit it.

If anything, by this point I am probably holding the first 20 spots in that line.

---

* Beyond, yes, the obvious fact that there are no other books like this in Infosec.
† So, you know … for the last time already, go get it!

Perhaps importantly, and to strip away the fourth wall for a moment, in some measure what this book has set out to do is to illustrate just how immature the field of Security truly is, still to this day, even as there are many* people running around out there speaking about it with a great deal of apparent sophistication, depth, and gravitas.

With a discipline that is this immature, the truth is that we are all still learning on the job.

And organizations still have generally little clue about how to understand, hire for, and manage the role of their Information Security leader.

I would like to note that there is indeed one more story that I would dearly love to share with you, and with the world at large, but sadly, it is one that I cannot. It is, in my opinion, worth an entire book all by itself, perhaps even a movie or better yet, a streaming series. It is both exciting and shocking at the same time, and also happens to be extremely relevant to today's world even though it happened a long time ago.

Alas, due to certain restrictions over which I have little to no control, it is a story that may remain untold forever, except as documented under seal in the various proceedings that had arisen from it over the years. It is, indeed, the best story I have.

But until such time as I am allowed to do so, all of these other tales will simply have to do. I hope you enjoyed them, maybe laughed at some, and cringed at others, perhaps even rolled your eyes here and there. I hope, in other words, that you were able to connect with them.

Because that would be my greatest reward.

—b

---

* Far, far too many.

Index